THE
COMPLETE
SPOKESPERSON

A workbook for managers
who meet the media

PETER BARTRAM·COLIN COULSON-THOMAS

KOGAN
PAGE

Kogan Page Limited
120 Pentonville Road
London N1 9JN

© Peter Bartram and Colin Coulson-Thomas 1991

British Library Cataloguing in Publication Data
A CIP record for this book is available from the British Library.

ISBN 0-7494-0492-2

Typeset by DP Photosetting, Aylesbury, Bucks
Printed and bound in Great Britain by
Biddles Ltd, Guildford and Kings Lynn

◀ Contents ▶

Using This Book

WHY A FRONT-LINE MANAGER NEEDS TO BE A COMPLETE SPOKESPERSON

'I'm a manager. My job is about managing the company, not hob-nobbing with journalists. Right?'

Right . . . and wrong. Your job is certainly about managing the company. But part of that also involves managing how your company is seen by outsiders. The public. Or, at least, that part of the public which is interested in your company. For at least part of its success will depend on how your company is seen by those outsiders.

Let's be blunt. Top managers can't duck the issue of facing up to the media any longer. But let's be fair. By choosing to read this book, you've already shown that at least *you* are not ducking the issue.

Today business is big news, getting more coverage than ever in the national press – including the tabloids – and on television and radio. Perhaps, like many managers, you take a jaundiced view of much of the media coverage of business. Ill-informed? Sensational? Only interested in bad news? Possibly you've echoed these criticisms like many other managers.

It is true that the media *is* interested in news that might be bad from one company's perspective. And there is also ill-informed and sensational comment to be found. But let's be quite clear. The media is also interested in good, positive news. The kind that makes PR people coo with delight. The news that can both build your company's reputation and contribute to its longer term 'bottom line' performance.

So what's the secret of getting across this good news? Often there is no secret. In case after case, it is because a manager has taken the time to sit down with a journalist and provide the information needed to write a strong positive story.

That's what this book is all about. It's about turning you into a manager who can create good news for your company.

As a manager you will have many skills, some of which you've consciously learned and others that you've acquired over the years. Perhaps you've never believed you needed to be a good spokesperson. But increasingly, you do. For apart from your specific tasks as a manager, you have two other duties to your company. One is to protect and enhance its image at all times. The other is to share in your company's social and moral responsibilities to society at large. And fulfilling both of these duties successfully will involve meeting the media.

So think again. With the burgeoning media coverage of business, most top managers now need spokesperson skills as part of their everyday management armoury. And those at the very top of their company need to focus as much on external communication as upon internal management. So, apart from the value to your company, building interpersonal and communication skills can enhance your career prospects.

Convinced? If you are not yet, we hope you will be by the time you reach the end of this book.

> **Remember . . .** the ability to put your company's case to the media is now a necessary – not an optional – skill for any front-line manager.

USING THE COMPLETE SPOKESPERSON

The aim of *The Complete Spokesperson* is to help you acquire spokesperson techniques and apply them in your own special circumstances. It has been designed so that you can apply the general lessons to the specific circumstances of your own organisation.

We've arranged the information in a way that helps you get to the essential points as quickly as possible. We've kept expositionary text to a minimum consistent with providing clear explanation and instruction.

There are three particular features of *The Complete Spokesperson* which are designed to make the book effective as a source of instruction and valuable as a long-term source of reference. They are as follows.

1. **Checklists** which are designed to summarise the main points now and provide a quick source of reference – an action programme – for the future.

2. **Remember** ... points which are designed to focus your attention on the really important issues. They are boxed and introduced with a lightbulb.

3. Data modules are designed for you to complete with information about your own company. Completing the data modules will ensure that you have absorbed the lessons of the book and will provide the essential material you need about your company to perform effectively as one of its spokespersons.

The Complete Spokesperson is not intended to be a manual on all public relations techniques. It does not set out to tell you how to mount a public relations campaign. That is a matter for public relations professionals. Instead, it focuses closely on those aspects of public relations activity that directors, partners and managers need to be personally involved with. That includes policy and planning issues as well as direct contact with journalists.

Public relations professionals will also find *The Complete Spokesperson* a useful tool for working with managers in identifying and disseminating messages and in preparing managers to meet the media.

THE LAYOUT OF THE COMPLETE SPOKESPERSON

The Complete Spokesperson has been arranged into nine main chapters (plus this introduction). Each has been designed as a self-contained unit dealing with a specific aspect of being a spokesperson.

First we advise you to read quickly through the whole book to get a general idea of the issues we deal with and their interrelation.

Then we suggest you study each of the chapters more closely, reacting to the questions we pose and filling in the Data Modules as they apply to your own organization.

The nine chapters cover the following topics:

- *understanding* the media;
- *identifying* your audiences;
- *defining* your corporate personality;
- *creating* your messages;
- *preparing* to meet the media;
- *meeting* the media;
- *appearing* on TV and radio;
- *communicating* in crisis;
- *learning* from experience.

When you have studied all the chapters you should be thoroughly prepared for your encounters with the media. And, if you have completed the Data Modules carefully, you will have created what amounts to a spokesperson's Bible for your organization.

Remember ... *The Complete Spokesperson* is more than a self-tuition course on meeting the media. It is a permanent source of reference on media policy for your organization.

◀ 1 ▶

Understanding The Media

'You cannot hope
to bribe or twist
thank God! the
British journalist.
But, seeing what
the man will do
Unbribed, there's
no occasion to.'

Humbert Wolfe in *The Uncelestial City*

In 'Understanding The Media' you'll learn about:

- the five reasons why your company needs spokespeople;

- three key roles you must perform as a spokesperson;

- how to find the kind of individual who makes the best spokesperson;

- the interview arena – how you and the journalist approach from different directions;

- the three kinds of interviews you'll have with journalists;

- what drives journalists – and how to turn it to your advantage.

THE FIVE REASONS WHY YOUR COMPANY NEEDS SPOKESPEOPLE

Your time is valuable. Why spend it with journalists? Why not leave it to your PR people? Isn't that what you pay them for?

The fact is that any public relations campaign can only be successful when it is a partnership: a partnership between the public relations professionals – whether in-house or from consultancies – and other senior decision-making managers.

Managers need to be involved because they understand the values, mission and objectives of their company better than anyone else. Public relations professionals need to be involved because their knowledge and experience can help guide the strategy and tactics of a PR campaign, and their training and skills can help put it into practice effectively and manage the campaign's activities.

In some cases, a public relations professional acts as his or her company's only official spokesperson. But, in many cases, that is not enough. There are still many occasions when other managers need to get into the front line and put their company's messages across.

CHECKLIST 1.1:
WHY MANAGERS NEED TO BE SPOKESPEOPLE

Knowledge

You know more about your company, or about your part of the company, than anyone else. Briefing an intermediary also takes time you can ill afford.

Authority

You are a senior person. What you say has the ring of authority. What helps to give you that authority is your position in the organization, the relevance of your experience and your expert knowledge.

Decision maker

You are a decision maker – and you can explain the reasons for those decisions better than those who were not involved in taking them.*

First hand

You are doing the job, facing the competition and meeting the customers. You have first-hand knowledge of all the circumstances, both within your company and outside it, that influence its decisions and policies.

Acceptable

In many cases, you are the only acceptable spokesperson to the media. They don't just want to interview PR people or junior staff.

* The British Institute of Management Report 'The Responsive Organization' (1989), based on a survey of 100 organizations employing three million people, found that companies are delegating more responsibility to individual managers. According to Sir John Harvey-Jones: 'Speed of decision making is critically important . . . decisions should be pushed down the organization. The aim should be for everyone to be responsible for their own work.'

THREE KEY ROLES YOU MUST PERFORM AS A SPOKESPERSON

So, as a manager and company spokesperson, just what is your role? This can be summed up under the three following headings.

1. *To set policy*

All too frequently, public relations activities are not closely enough related to company vision, mission and objectives. In conjunction with other managers, including public relations professionals, your task is to make sure your company has a PR policy that matches your corporate mission and objectives. The importance of this was discovered by a director of a multinational company who called a meeting of the management team to discuss why so little was achieved for the money spent on public relations consultancy. He said: 'We concluded there was nothing wrong with the quality of the external resource. It was just not being used properly. To turn the potential represented by the expertise into reality in terms of results, what is needed is direction, leadership and specific objectives.'

2. *To formulate the messages*

In conjunction with other managers and your public relations advisers, you need to decide what messages will help your company achieve its corporate objectives. And how they will be best put across. After all, as a spokesperson you will need to feel comfortable with those messages. They will be taken as, and should be, *your* messages.

3. *To lead your PR team over the top*

As we have seen, there is a limit to what public relations professionals can achieve without top management involvement. You must talk to the media. And take your place in the front-line. In doing that, you will provide a focus for your company's public relations – and pave the way for the PR department's other activities.

> **Remember ...** talking to journalists is the most effective way of communicating your messages to them and building a long-term understanding which is the foundation and should be a purpose of all good media campaigns.

HOW TO FIND THE KIND OF INDIVIDUAL WHO MAKES THE BEST SPOKESPERSON

Who in your company would make the best spokesperson? Perhaps you need more than one spokesperson. In a large company with many divisions that will certainly be the case. But, whatever your situation, each spokesperson will need to have a blend of two kinds of qualities:

- relevant work experience; and

- helpful personal qualities.

CHECKLIST 1.2:
QUALITIES NEEDED BY SPOKESPEOPLE

Work experience

Your ideal spokesperson should:

- understand and be committed to the vision, mission and strategy of the company and the key requirements for success;

- have first-hand knowledge, at a senior level, of the business;

- have a broadly based understanding of the business as a whole;

- have contributed to the formulation of the PR strategy that will support your company mission and objectives;

- have experience of more than one function in the business in order to be able to take a balanced perspective;

- be able to take an outward looking view of your company and the part it plays in its industry and society generally;

- have the time to perform the duties of a spokesperson in addition to other work;

- consider those duties as a key element of his or her responsibilities rather than just 'something extra' to do.

Personal qualities

Your ideal spokesperson should:

- be sensitive and responsive to the values, concerns and interests of others;*

- have a friendly, outgoing personality;**

- be articulate, but not verbose (as George Eliot put it: 'Blessed is the man who, having nothing to say, abstains from giving in words evidence of the fact');

* The British Institute of Management Report 'Beyond Quality' (1990) suggests that customers are increasingly assuming reliability and performance in products. 'Softer' requirements, such as 'look' and 'feel' are becoming more important. Customers may select suppliers – and people their employers – because of the values they represent. The report suggests that a new breed of sensitive and more responsive manager is needed, able to identify, empathize with and respond to values and feelings.

** One blue-chip company selected its chairman from the shortlist of available candidates largely on the basis of skill and warmth as an external communicator. The chief executive explained: 'At this level, it's assumed that people are good managers. A spokesman personifies the company. We want to come across as caring and feeling, not hard and tough. The "Dallas" type is out. Warm human beings are in.'

- have a good speaking voice (especially important for radio and TV);

- be of smart appearance, and for TV at least, look fairly 'normal' (as TV is heavily about images). However, you don't have to be a Robert Redford or Marilyn Monroe look-alike;

- have pleasant behaviour in social situations (for example, people who smoke insensitively, drink excessively or swear unrestrainedly can be an embarrassment);

- have the enthusiasm to be a spokesperson.

It is also helpful if the spokesperson is as senior within the organization as possible. It adds to his or her credibility. But it is not always the case that the most senior manager, either of a company or department, makes the best spokesperson. According to a survey ('The Effective Board', 1991) of 218 company directors – chairpersons and chief executives – carried out by Adaptation Ltd for the Institute of Directors, 'communications skills' was one of the top three qualities sought in new appointments to the board. It also featured as one of the top ten specific competencies in the training and development of directors.

However, there may be cases when only the top person will do. And if that is the case he or she should try to develop all the qualities needed when called on to be a spokesperson.

THE INTERVIEW ARENA – HOW YOU AND THE JOURNALIST APPROACH FROM DIFFERENT DIRECTIONS

Journalist – friend or foe? The answer is actually neither. He or she is a professional with a job to do. This may involve him or her writing about your company in situations which can be either helpful or unhelpful to you.

Whichever is the case, you should treat him or her like any other business contact. And, remember, he or she is also likely to respond like any external business contact. There is no need to fawn or ingratiate yourself. You certainly shouldn't treat the journalist like something the cat dragged in, either. Just adopt your usual good business manners and remember Stanislaus's advice: 'To be vain of one's rank or place is to show that one is beneath it.'

What are journalists like? Well, Hollywood got it wrong. There is no such stereotype of the hard drinking journalist with a trench coat and trilby. In fact, jounalists are in the business for a variety of motives. Some like the lifestyle, others have a passion for the subjects they write about. Some have ideals about seeking and publishing truth, others treat it as a nine-to-five job. Over a period of time you're likely to meet many types.

In any specialized area of journalism you may meet writers who have an encyclopaedic knowledge of their subjects. There are others, perhaps new to the business, who've barely mastered the first principles. In quite a few cases, you will meet journalists who need help in understanding the context of a story.

As people, they cover as broad a cross-section of humankind as the rest of the population. There is nothing special about them. However, it *is* worth mentioning that journalism does tend to have more than its fair share of 'characters'. Former newspaper proprietor, the late Lord Thomson once said: 'It is part of the social mission of every newspaper to provide a refuge and a home for the largest number of salaried eccentrics.'

There are two qualities that all good journalists do have in common. First, they are anxious to preserve their independence and integrity. Secondly, they are sensitive to being manipulated.

As you meet journalists in the arena of the interview, you should understand that you both approach from different directions. Appreciating the differences will help you to understand the nature of your task as a spokesperson.

Let's examine these two directions.

CHECKLIST 1.3: WHAT MANAGERS AND JOURNALISTS BRING TO AN INTERVIEW

MANAGERS	JOURNALISTS
DOERS – you're paid to take decisions and manage	OBSERVERS – they're paid to watch and write
LONG TERM – you plan ahead	SHORT TERM – the horizon is the next deadline
SUBJECTIVE – your life is entwined with your company*	OBJECTIVE – they view your company as outsiders
ENTHUSIASTIC – you have a passion for your company and its products	DISPASSIONATE – they have no emotional feeling for the company. They want a good story
RATIONAL – you're trained to think about management problems in a logical and structured way	INTUITIVE – a good journalist has a 'nose' for a story
DIFFUSED – as a busy manager you have many tasks – talking to journalists is just one preoccupation	FOCUSED – writing a given story is the one task in hand for the journalist interviewing you
SPECIALIST – you may have studied a specialist management discipline – and may know more about it than anyone else in your company**	GENERALIST – the writer may be a general assignment reporter – and even a specialist will not match your knowledge in respect of your company

* It is enough if you can say, like Goethe: 'I can promise to be candid, though I may not be impartial.'

** Take this advice: 'If you have knowledge, let others light their candles by it.' (Margaret Fuller).

MANAGERS	JOURNALISTS
DEPTH – you know about your company, products and industry in detail	BREADTH – the journalist sees many companies and situations. His knowledge may be a mile wide but an inch deep
SENSITIVE – you will be concerned about the way your company is described and the interpretation others may put on the words used	INDIFFERENT – the journalist writes the story as he sees it without reference to your feelings
RESPONSIBLE – you may work within a hierarchy, constrained by policies and procedures	INDEPENDENT – the journalist has editorial freedom, especially when a specialist correspondent or freelance
MEANS – for you a story is not an end in itself – it is a way of helping to achieve a business objective	END – for the journalist, the aim is to get a story into print or on the air

THE THREE KINDS OF INTERVIEWS YOU'LL HAVE WITH JOURNALISTS

You will find that you will be interviewed in broadly three kinds of situations.

- The first is when you or your PR people have set up an interview with a journalist for a specific purpose. We will call this the **proactive** interview.

- The second is when you are responding to requests for information from a journalist, either about a topic concerning your company or about something he or she thinks you might have useful information or views on. We will call this the **reactive** interview.

- The third is when you are responding to requests for information as a result of a train of events deeply affecting your company, but significantly outside its control. We will call this the **crisis** interview. (Communicating in crisis is dealt with specifically in Chapter 8.)

It is important to understand the frameworks in which each of these kinds of interview takes place.

CHECKLIST 1.4:
FEATURES OF THE PROACTIVE INTERVIEW

The proactive interview:

- takes place at your invitation;

- on a subject of your choosing;

- normally in favourable circumstances;

- usually at your choice of location;

- at a convenient time;

- often face to face;

- with a friendly (or at least not overtly hostile) journalist;

- asking probing but not hostile questions;

- for an article or programme that may not be too time-critical.

But ... the journalist may seek to 'hijack' the opportunity to pursue another topic.

CHECKLIST 1.5:
FEATURES OF THE REACTIVE INTERVIEW

The reactive interview:

- takes place at the journalist's request;

- on a topic he or she raises;

- in possibly unfavourable circumstances;

- at a place of his or her choosing;

- at a time that may not be convenient;

- or (usually) over the telephone;

- with a journalist motivated to pursue a story of his or her own choosing;

- with questions that may be inconvenient or hostile;

- for an article or programme that may be time-critical.

But ... you could score by aiding the journalist with a helpful message that is relevant to the story.

CHECKLIST 1.6:
FEATURES OF THE CRISIS INTERVIEW

The crisis interview:

- takes place at the journalist's insistence;

- under often unfavourable circumstances;

- on the subject of the crisis;

- about which you may not have full information;

- in a situation that could be changing rapidly;

- with questions that could be inconvenient, embarrassing or hostile;

- for news media whose deadlines may be minutes away;

- or, in some cases, for live transmission.

But . . . by being prepared and remaining calm, you can show you are in control of the situation.

WHAT DRIVES JOURNALISTS – AND HOW TO TURN IT TO YOUR ADVANTAGE

What makes journalists tick? They are professionals with a job to do and – as in most other kinds of business – the ones that get on are those that enjoy what they do and do it best.

Whether a journalist wants a full-scale interview or just a simple piece of information, you can score by helping him or her to do their job better.

We will now look at four driving forces in journalists' lives and show how, by reacting intelligently to them, you can help the journalist, and thus achieve better and more positive press coverage for your company. (Incidentally, these are not the only driving forces in journalists' lives, but they're common to most.)

Briefly, the four driving forces are:

● serving readers well;

● getting a good story;

● beating rival publications (or programmes);

● hitting deadlines.

Serving readers well

Only one thing makes a commercially successful publication – readers. Or, in the case of radio and TV, listeners and viewers. Without readers there will be no sales revenue (if the publication is sold) and without readers, listeners and viewers there will certainly be little advertising revenue.

Successful publications – and successful journalists – know what their readers want to read. The journalist's primary task is meeting the needs of his or her readers, rather than helping you to put your message across.

In a speech given in 1988 to the Institute of Public Relations, John Pullin, editor of *The Engineer*, gave this advice: 'The starting point for any publication is its readers. The kind of information with which we regale our readers is, we hope, of two sorts – the kind which will enable them to do their jobs better, and the kind which will make them better, finer, more rounded people.' Further, one magazine publisher takes a hard-nosed approach when reviewing his company's periodical titles. He said: 'I will ask what will happen if I close this title down. What, if anything, will the readers miss? What won't they be able to do without? This helps me to focus on the strengths and weaknesses of individual publications.'

If you plan to meet a journalist, make sure you understand the *content, treatment* and *style* of the publication he or she is writing for or the radio or TV programme. Then adapt your message to match those three main criteria.

● **Content** is about what's in the publication or on the radio or TV programme. In other words, the subject matter. For example, are there regular 'departments' or columns in the publication or programme dealing with specific topics? Michael Bland Communications Consultancy publishes *PR Opportunities in the National Press* annually, which analyzes the contents of the main national newspapers based on more than 25,000 individual news items. The publication analyzes the media's latest vogue themes. Contact the consultancy at Fossett Lane, Fordham, Colchester, Essex CO6 3NZ.

- **Treatment** is about how that subject matter is dealt with. What level is it pitched at? For example, is it general or specialist? Purely factual or opinionated? Is it overlaid with the publication's or programme's point of view? Does it have lots of examples and quotes? For example, the *Food and Drink* programme on BBC 2 frequently mentions a wide range of food and drinks products – but takes a strong editorial line on them. It either loves them or hates them. It is strongly influenced by the wholesomeness of the product, its consumer appeal and its value for money.

- **Style** is about how the material is presented. For example, are there lots of pictures, and if so of what? Does the publication or programme use cartoons, graphs, technical drawings? Has the publication or programme been styled to appeal to a particular audience? There would be no point, for instance, in trying to get a photograph of your company chairman into the *Wall Street Journal* since it doesn't carry photographs.

Getting a good story

Journalists don't actually shout 'hold the front page', but a strong story, especially an exclusive, still makes the adrenalin pump faster. It's always difficult to interest journalists in a tired old piece of information. But it's never hard to interest them in a genuinely 'good' story.

So, if you have what you consider to be a 'good' story – one that you're certain they'll go for, *and* which serves your corporate objectives – consider carefully how to make the most of it. You need to market your story effectively. For example, there might be one main publication that covers the audience you want to reach. You might gain most coverage by giving the story to that one publication – the fact that the story is exclusive increases its value to that publication.

Alternatively, there may be several publications – each with a different focus – that reach your targeted audience. Tailor your story to each. And divide the story up. Try to make sure that each publication gets a bit of exclusivity.

But a word of caution. In the long run, you must be seen by journalists to be fair and even-handed. Journalists can resent favouritism – especially when they're on the wrong end of it. In a market served by several rival publications, they should all receive fair treatment from you.

Beating rival publications

Newspapers and magazines are commercial organizations like any other business and are in competition with one another. Journalists generally relish the competitive cut and thrust involved in beating rival publications to a story. And they are not just playing games – at worst, their jobs can be at stake.

One area where there is especially keen competition is in the 'quality' Sunday newspaper market. There are now four competitors – *Sunday Times, Observer, Sunday Telegraph* and *Independent on Sunday*. Although on a typical Sunday, all four will be chasing at least a dozen of the same stories, they all need a 'unique' angle. At the margin, they are bidding for the same readers, yet they must differentiate themselves in order to build reader loyalty.

There are times when you can turn this to your advantage. For instance, if you're known as a reliable and interesting source of comment about your industry, there could be times when you can help a newspaper scrambling to catch up with a rival that has got a story it missed by providing new facts, background information or informed comment.

That paper will be looking for a new angle or fresh material in order to take the story further – for example, by putting it in a broader context or perspective. Or it may be seeking to 'rubbish' the rival's story. Being available and having something useful to say can put you into the news in a way that can be helpful to your company.

It does not matter that the original story was not your own. The door may even have been opened by a competitor. But if you have information that can take the story further, or provide a better example, you can secure valuable coverage for your company.

Hitting deadlines

Time is a tyrant for most managers. But in no industry is this more the case than in radio or television, or in newspaper publishing.

When a story is breaking, a journalist needs information and comment fast – it could be in a matter of minutes. If you become known as a spokesperson who provides reliable information quickly, journalists will turn to you. And you could receive positive and helpful coverage for your company.

The converse is also true. The biggest story since the Second World War arriving after the presses have started to roll will not make it to the paper. (Although it might make it to the next edition if it is a morning or evening paper with several editions.) But, in the case of the majority of trade newspapers or magazines that only have one edition a week or a month, if it isn't a big story, it may be too stale to use by the next issue. In journalism the truism 'Tomorrow is another day' holds sway.

Remember ... understanding what drives journalists, and being genuinely helpful – even when there doesn't seem to be any immediate publicity pay-off for you – will build a fund of goodwill that could eventually translate into more positive coverage for your company.

TO SUM UP

In this chapter you've:

- learned about five reasons why your company needs managers who can act effectively as spokespeople;

- discovered the three key roles you can play as a spokesperson;

- found out about the work experience and personal qualities that make a good spokesperson;

- seen how you and the journalist will approach any interview from totally different directions;

- found out about the different characteristics of proactive, reactive and crisis interviews;

- learned about four driving forces in journalists' lives – and how you can turn them to your company's benefit.

◀ 2 ▶

Identifying Your Audiences

'There is only one thing in the world worse than being talked about, and that is not being talked about.'

Oscar Wilde, The Picture of Dorian Gray

In 'Identifying Your Audiences' you'll learn about:

○ how to find the starting post for your corporate communications campaign;

○ two issues you must address to reach your target audiences;

○ how to pinpoint the people you really need to reach;

○ 15 media arenas from which to choose channels to reach your target audiences;

○ how to make the human factor work in your favour.

HOW TO FIND THE STARTING POST FOR YOUR CORPORATE COMMUNICATIONS CAMPAIGN

Many corporate communications and public relations campaigns fail. Too many. And they do so because they have not been planned with enough care.

Henry Ford knew what he was talking about when he said: 'Thinking is the hardest work there is, which is the probable reason why so few engage in it.'

Everything you do in your company – almost everything, at any rate – should serve your company's mission and help it to achieve its business objectives. Communication is no exception.

So, just what is the starting point? You have decided you need to communicate more effectively. But to whom? And, even more fundamentally, why? Until you have answered these questions, you cannot decide *what* you are going to communicate. Communicating without thinking can actually reduce the influence you have on the people you are seeking to reach. The well-known director general of a national business organization, who had been sounding off in ever more extreme terms about government policies, was quietly slipped the gypsy's warning by a senior civil servant. Said the civil servant: 'I can understand why you talk to the press. The members like to see references to their association in the media. But it's always easier to get column inches by criticizing things. By being constantly critical, you make it difficult for my colleagues to see you as the source of balanced and authoritative representations.' Motto: Know who you're trying to influence and why.

From a practical point of view, managers often first realize they need to communicate more effectively with people around them and in the outside world when they come face to face with a specific problem. It could, for example, be:

- falling sales of a flagship product;

- an inability to penetrate a new market;

- difficulty in differentiating the company or a product from that of competitors;

- failure to attract quality or specialized staff;

- constraints on business success applied by governments or other public bodies.

And, of course, there are many, many other specific business problems that could cause you to look at the effectiveness of your communications.

As you can see, all these problems – and the many other examples that could be mentioned – have a specific focus. And in almost all cases the problem arises from failing to communicate effectively with specific groups of people – we'll call them 'audiences'.

So the starting post is to decide which audiences you need to reach in order to achieve your business objectives. This is what we will deal with in this chapter. Then in Chapter 3, we'll decide how you can best shape your corporate personality to serve those business objectives. And in Chapter 4 we'll work out how to devise messages that can effectively reach your target audiences and serve your business objectives.

But before you start to focus your mind on your audiences, you need to refresh your memory about your specific business objectives. And you need to identify any specific problems which demand improved communications.

Remember ... the purpose of communication is to reach those audiences that can help your company to fulfil its mission and achieve its specific business objectives with effective messages.

TWO ISSUES YOU MUST ADDRESS TO REACH YOUR TARGET AUDIENCES

You have now established that, in order to achieve your business objectives or to overcome specific problems, you need to communicate effectively with your target audiences. Depending on the size of your company, that could mean a lot of people in many different walks of life. Your time is valuable. You must use it effectively. And that means recognizing you can't communicate with all of the people all of the time. So you need to identify those audiences who are most important – and target your messages at them. Those important audiences can be both *outside* and *inside* your company.

In fact, you face two main issues in seeking to reach your chosen audiences.

- **You need to decide who your audiences are.** Don't believe that you can reach everyone. In any event, a message that is aimed at everyone is often of interest to no-one. Besides, no company needs to reach everyone. Only the Pope addresses all of mankind. Remember, the people out there who might be interested in your message are only half listening. They don't sit around waiting for pearls of wisdom to drop from your lips. They've got other matters on their minds. If you say something that is half interesting to them, they might prick up their ears and take notice. But it must be of real interest – and it must be aimed at *them*.

- **You need to select the most effective channels for conveying your messages to these different audiences.** In most cases, you'll be reaching your audiences through third-party intermediaries – newspapers, magazines, and radio and TV programmes. You can also create your own channels, by the use of customer or staff newsletters or magazines. So you need to decide which are likely to be the most effective.

HOW TO PINPOINT THE PEOPLE YOU REALLY NEED TO REACH

You are trying to reach people who can influence your company's business success. These normally fall into the following three main categories.

1. Production audiences

These are people who help to make, distribute and sell your products and services. They include:

- management;
- staff;
- sales team;
- suppliers;
- dealers/distributors;
- retailers.

2. End-user audiences

These are people who use or could use your products or services. They include:

- customers;
- potential customers;
- rival's customers;
- non-users.

3. Influencer audiences

These are people who help to create the business and social climate in which your company operates. They include:

- local communities;
- government/public bodies;
- elected officials;
- investors;
- special interest groups;
- educational institutions.

The interesting thing about press coverage is that it often produces a 'self-selecting' response. A manager who had got some coverage for his company in the *Financial Times*, made this comment: 'It's interesting who is responding. I'm hearing from those who are interested, rather than mailing cold to those I think are interested. I've got some good leads. Some of them I wouldn't have thought of, but now that they have approached us, I can see that our services can really help them.'

Data Module 1 lists the different groups of people that could be relevant as targets for your messages. Not all of them will be relevant and some will be more important than others.

Scan the list. Then work through it and tick the level of relevance of each of the target groups from the point of view of your company, your business objectives and your communications problems.

DATA MODULE 1: A PRIORITIZED PROFILE OF TARGET AUDIENCES FOR YOUR COMPANY

Rating: [E]ssential/[I]mportant/[U]seful/[N]ot [R]elevant

Production audiences:	E	I	U	NR
1 Management	[ ]	[ ]	[ ]	[ ]
2 Staff	[ ]	[ ]	[ ]	[ ]
3 Sales team	[ ]	[ ]	[ ]	[ ]
4 Suppliers	[ ]	[ ]	[ ]	[ ]
5 Dealers/distributors	[ ]	[ ]	[ ]	[ ]
6 Retailers	[ ]	[ ]	[ ]	[ ]
7 Others . . .	[ ]	[ ]	[ ]	[ ]
(specify)	[ ]	[ ]	[ ]	[ ]

End-user audiences:	E	I	U	NR
8 Customers	[ ]	[ ]	[ ]	[ ]
9 Potential customers	[ ]	[ ]	[ ]	[ ]
10 Rival's customers	[ ]	[ ]	[ ]	[ ]
11 Non-users	[ ]	[ ]	[ ]	[ ]
12 Others . . .	[ ]	[ ]	[ ]	[ ]
(specify)	[ ]	[ ]	[ ]	[ ]

Influencer audiences:	E	I	U	NR
13 Local communities	[ ]	[ ]	[ ]	[ ]
14 Govt/public bodies	[ ]	[ ]	[ ]	[ ]
15 Elected officials	[ ]	[ ]	[ ]	[ ]
16 Investors	[ ]	[ ]	[ ]	[ ]
17 Special interests	[ ]	[ ]	[ ]	[ ]
18 Educational institutions	[ ]	[ ]	[ ]	[ ]
19 Others . . .	[ ]	[ ]	[ ]	[ ]
(specify)	[ ]	[ ]	[ ]	[ ]

(*NB:* For each audience, tick the column that is most relevant.)

When you have completed Data Module 1, you will have a reasonable idea of your highest priorities. Yet you need to be even more precise if you are to score a high proportion of bullseyes in your corporate communications programme.

By glancing down each column of Data Module 1, you can see broadly where your essential, important and useful audiences are located.

You have now described *what* your target audiences are. You have not yet described *who* they are. To target with true precision, you need to be more specific about this. Data Module 2 has been designed to help you in this process.

In Data Module 2, take each of the categories in Data Module 1 that you marked as 'essential'. Now for each of those categories, describe as precisely as you can who those people are. (You can repeat the process for the 'important' and 'useful' categories if you feel it is necessary.) For example, if you have marked an E against 'Rival's customers' you could write something like: 'Existing users of MS-DOS based accounting software' or 'People who have bought a pair of tennis shoes in the last year'.

It is important that you should make your descriptions:

- broad enough to include all people who could be of interest to you in that category; and

- narrow enough to produce a clear focus and exclude those people who really are of no or only very small concern to you.

> **Remember ...** the more precise and selective you are in defining your target audiences, the more successful your communications are likely to be. You will be able to develop messages that most persuasively reach your target audiences and you will use your limited resources to the best effect.

DATA MODULE 2: DESCRIPTIONS OF TARGET AUDIENCES

Production audiences:

1. Management	
2. Staff	
3. Sales team	
4. Suppliers	
5. Dealers/distributors	
6. Retailers	
7. Others	

End-user audiences:	
8. Customers	
9. Potential customers	
10. Rivals' customers	
11. Non-users	
12. Others	

Influencer audiences:	
13. Local communities	
14. Government/public bodies	
15. Elected officials	
16. Investors	
17. Special interest groups	
18. Educational institutions	
19. Others	

(When you have completed this and Data Module 1, you should have clearly defined those audiences which are the highest priorities for your corporate communications campaign.)

THE 15 MEDIA ARENAS FROM WHICH TO CHOOSE CHANNELS TO REACH YOUR TARGET AUDIENCES

Now that you have decided on the people you most want to reach with your messages, the next task is to decide on the best means of reaching them. In other words, you need to identify the channels you will use.

You have the whole UK media from which to choose. The whole overseas media, too, if you are concerned to project your message to foreign markets.

The key to your success is selectivity. There are more than 15,000 regularly published newspapers, magazines and periodicals in the UK. More than a hundred radio stations. More than twenty television stations. But you don't have unlimited time to devote to meeting the media. So priorities are important. Selection is essential.

You have three tasks to perform.

- First, you need to identify those newspapers, magazines and broadcast programmes whose circulations or audiences most closely match the audiences you are seeking to reach.*

- Secondly, you need to match your specific audiences to specific target publications. In other words, you need the right channel for each audience.

- Thirdly, you need to introduce the human factor. You must identify the individuals – reporters or broadcasters – on your target media who are the people you need to reach. In the final analysis, it is people you have to talk to.

* A book publisher found that half of his sales of a specialist report came from one mention in *The Sunday Times*. He said: 'I've had more than 400 enquiries so far. It's the same with the reports we publish. I don't bother to read the press cuttings any more. I know when we have a mention – the phone starts ringing and the sales go up.'

CHECKLIST 2.1: THE DIFFERENT MEDIA ARENAS

There are 15 main arenas in which to locate the publications or programmes that will provide you with the best chances of reaching your audiences:

- international media;
- national newspapers;
- regional newspapers;
- local newspapers;
- consumer magazines;
- business magazines;
- professional magazines;
- trade and technical press;
- newsletters;
- national television;
- regional television;
- national radio;
- local radio;
- databases/electronic media; and
- company produced publications.

International media

Includes newspapers and specialist magazines with overseas circulations, such as the *Financial Times* and *The Economist*, and the European edition of the *Wall Street Journal*, and the World Service of the BBC. It should be noted that many professional and technical publications produced by or in conjunction with associations have surprisingly high overseas circulations.

National newspapers

Includes daily and Sunday papers. Many of them run specialist sections on subjects ranging from computers to fashion, from business to gardening. At the quality end of the market, an important trend of the last few years has been towards 'departmentalization'. The *Guardian* has led the way with separate sections each week for education, media and technology, among other subjects. But other papers are following to a greater or lesser degree.

Regional newspapers

Includes morning and evening papers. Always a strong regional bias, and with a special interest in industries and companies with a firm local base. Regional morning papers have been showing declining circulations for some years, but evening papers still hold their own. Many regional papers are owned by chains with specialist London correspondents – including business and City correspondents – who contribute to all papers in the chain.

Local newspapers

Includes paid-for and freesheets (a fast growing section of the market). Totally concerned with local issues, including local business.

Consumer magazines

The kinds of magazines you see on a newsagent's rack. Includes specialist magazines for women, leisure interests, sports and hobbies, plus political and cultural activities. In the face of growing media competition, consumer magazines are becoming increasingly tightly targeted. For instance, it is no longer enough to produce a 'woman's' magazine. Such a magazine has to be aimed precisely at a segment of women readers and reflect their concerns, interests and lifestyles. This makes it important to look beneath the surface to see precisely who reads a given publication.

Business magazines

Includes some magazines on open distribution and some on subscription or controlled circulation. Includes general business publications with national or international circulations and regional business publications.

The business magazine market is dominated by two giants: *Management Today* and *The Director*, both available on controlled circulation or by subscription. *Business*, a glossy that is a British-style *Fortune*, is available on bookstalls. Out in the provinces there is a thick undergrowth of regional business magazines and local Chamber of Commerce publications.

Professional magazines

Includes publications aimed at specific professional groups, such as doctors, architects, accountants or solicitors. Often produced in conjunction with a professional association.

Accountants to zoologists all have their own professional or scientific publications which are normally required reading. But in cases where a profession is served by more than one publication – lawyers and doctors, for example – each has its own individual focus.

Trade and technical press

Mostly vertical market publications dealing with a special interest or user group. You name it, and there'll be a publication for it. From bookselling to woodwork and from grocery to electronics.

Newsletters

Small circulation, specialist niche publications which often reach high-quality audiences in their chosen subject areas.

The newsletter market is not as highly developed in the UK as in the US, but newsletters reach small, highly targeted and often influential markets. Top newsletter areas are stocks and shares, energy, technology.

National television

Four terrestrial channels plus satellite channels. Vast range of programming, but growing number of niche programmes which offer opportunities for companies to provide material.

There is a growing range of specialist business programming. Channel 4's *Business Daily* is broadcast every day from Monday to Friday. City news is updated by the BBC's *Business Breakfast* team every day from Monday to Friday. There are plenty of other opportunities – a lucky break on *Jim'll Fix It* can be worth thousands!

Regional television

Fifteen regional ITV companies with a duty to provide strong news coverage of their regions. And the BBC also has a strong regional structure – there are three national regions (Northern Ireland, Scotland and Wales) and five English regions (Midlands, North East, North West, South and East, and South and West). Many produce own news and/or magazine programmes that are interested in regional business.

National radio

Five BBC channels. Radios 2 and 4 in particular offer a range of specialist programmes with opportunities for coverage of aspects of business. Radio 4's *Six O'Clock News* is particularly strong on business news. There is a wide range of other specialist programming. Magazine programmes, such as *Woman's Hour*, are constantly looking for strong, relevant ideas.

Local radio

More than a hundred BBC and independent stations with a strong appetite for stories relating to their audience areas. Because local radio generally uses a fairly loosely structured programming approach, it has a more flexible format. Local radio stations are always interested in strong local news, and there are more opportunities for interviews and even talks. Local stations occasionally use pre-recorded tapes – but only when the topic is of local relevance and the tape is not too commercial in approach.

Databases/electronic media

Increasingly important as a source of instant desktop reference in a wide range of industries and professions. A growing number of managers now get information from teletext or on-line information providers who deliver their services to desktop terminals.

Company produced publications

Designed and targeted to reach selected internal or external audiences. This, again, is a growth market place. The top publications – American Express's *Expressions* or *Departure*, National Westminster's *Dimensions*, BUPA's *Upbeat* – now rival publications on the bookstalls.

The media arenas described above are your potential channels of communication. You now need to match these channels to the different audiences you have already identified.

This is a task which requires some care. In any sophisticated corporate communications campaign, different messages will be aimed at different audiences. Some messages may be right for one audience, but not for another. You need to make sure that each message is satisfactorily targeted. The best way to do that is to ensure that channels are carefully chosen.

Data Module 3 is designed to help you make these choices. It is laid out as a matrix. (To make it easier to use it is divided into sections, one for each of the three main audience areas.)

To complete this matrix follow this procedure.

- First, in the brackets under each audience (ie 'Management') mark the importance rating you assigned to it in Module 1 (ie E for 'essential', etc).

- Secondly, for each audience run down the column and against each media arena assess its importance for that audience. (Use the same rating system as for Module 1: E = essential; I = important; U = useful; NR = not relevant.)

- Thirdly, by identifying those squares on the matrix where an 'E' audience is matched by an 'E' media rating, you will be able to see where your priorities lie.

DATA MODULE 3: MATCHING YOUR PRIORITY AUDIENCES TO THE MOST EFFECTIVE COMMUNICATIONS CHANNELS

Production audiences:	1 Management [ ]	2 Staff [ ]	3 Sales [ ]	4 Suppliers [ ]	5 Distributors [ ]	6 Retail [ ]	7 Others [ ]
International media	[ ]	[ ]	[ ]	[ ]	[ ]	[ ]	[ ]
National newspaper	[ ]	[ ]	[ ]	[ ]	[ ]	[ ]	[ ]
Regional newspaper	[ ]	[ ]	[ ]	[ ]	[ ]	[ ]	[ ]
Local newspaper	[ ]	[ ]	[ ]	[ ]	[ ]	[ ]	[ ]
Consumer magazine	[ ]	[ ]	[ ]	[ ]	[ ]	[ ]	[ ]
Business magazine	[ ]	[ ]	[ ]	[ ]	[ ]	[ ]	[ ]
Professional magazine	[ ]	[ ]	[ ]	[ ]	[ ]	[ ]	[ ]
Trade and technical	[ ]	[ ]	[ ]	[ ]	[ ]	[ ]	[ ]
Newsletter	[ ]	[ ]	[ ]	[ ]	[ ]	[ ]	[ ]
National television	[ ]	[ ]	[ ]	[ ]	[ ]	[ ]	[ ]
Regional television	[ ]	[ ]	[ ]	[ ]	[ ]	[ ]	[ ]
National radio	[ ]	[ ]	[ ]	[ ]	[ ]	[ ]	[ ]
Local radio	[ ]	[ ]	[ ]	[ ]	[ ]	[ ]	[ ]
Database/ electronic	[ ]	[ ]	[ ]	[ ]	[ ]	[ ]	[ ]
Company publication	[ ]	[ ]	[ ]	[ ]	[ ]	[ ]	[ ]

End-user audiences:	8 Customers [ ]	9 Potential customers [ ]	10 Rival customers [ ]	11 Non-users [ ]	12 Others [ ]
International media	[ ]	[ ]	[ ]	[ ]	[ ]
National newspaper	[ ]	[ ]	[ ]	[ ]	[ ]
Regional newspaper	[ ]	[ ]	[ ]	[ ]	[ ]
Local newspaper	[ ]	[ ]	[ ]	[ ]	[ ]
Consumer magazine	[ ]	[ ]	[ ]	[ ]	[ ]
Business magazine	[ ]	[ ]	[ ]	[ ]	[ ]
Professional magazine	[ ]	[ ]	[ ]	[ ]	[ ]
Trade and technical	[ ]	[ ]	[ ]	[ ]	[ ]
Newsletter	[ ]	[ ]	[ ]	[ ]	[ ]
National television	[ ]	[ ]	[ ]	[ ]	[ ]
Regional television	[ ]	[ ]	[ ]	[ ]	[ ]
National radio	[ ]	[ ]	[ ]	[ ]	[ ]
Local radio	[ ]	[ ]	[ ]	[ ]	[ ]
Database/ electronic	[ ]	[ ]	[ ]	[ ]	[ ]
Company publication	[ ]	[ ]	[ ]	[ ]	[ ]

Influencer audiences:	13 Local comm [ ]	14 Government bodies [ ]	15 Elected officials [ ]	16 Investors [ ]	17 Special interest [ ]	18 Educational institutions [ ]	19 Other [ ]
International media	[ ]	[ ]	[ ]	[ ]	[ ]	[ ]	[ ]
National newspaper	[ ]	[ ]	[ ]	[ ]	[ ]	[ ]	[ ]
Regional newspaper	[ ]	[ ]	[ ]	[ ]	[ ]	[ ]	[ ]
Local newspaper	[ ]	[ ]	[ ]	[ ]	[ ]	[ ]	[ ]
Consumer magazine	[ ]	[ ]	[ ]	[ ]	[ ]	[ ]	[ ]
Business magazine	[ ]	[ ]	[ ]	[ ]	[ ]	[ ]	[ ]
Professional magazine	[ ]	[ ]	[ ]	[ ]	[ ]	[ ]	[ ]
Trade and technical	[ ]	[ ]	[ ]	[ ]	[ ]	[ ]	[ ]
Newsletter	[ ]	[ ]	[ ]	[ ]	[ ]	[ ]	[ ]
National television	[ ]	[ ]	[ ]	[ ]	[ ]	[ ]	[ ]
Regional television	[ ]	[ ]	[ ]	[ ]	[ ]	[ ]	[ ]
National radio	[ ]	[ ]	[ ]	[ ]	[ ]	[ ]	[ ]
Local radio	[ ]	[ ]	[ ]	[ ]	[ ]	[ ]	[ ]
Database/ electronic	[ ]	[ ]	[ ]	[ ]	[ ]	[ ]	[ ]
Company publication	[ ]	[ ]	[ ]	[ ]	[ ]	[ ]	[ ]

You have now identified the main target media arenas where you want to concentrate your attack. But you must be more precise. You need to match your specific audiences to the publications and programmes that will help you reach them.

In order to do that, you need to get a clear idea of the individual publications or programmes in each of your priority media channels. You need to research – or get your PR professionals to research – the key publications in each of your priority sectors.

There are a number of publications that can help you do this. They include the following.

CHECKLIST 2.2: SOURCES OF MEDIA INFORMATION

PIMS UK Media Directory

Contains lists of publications in different categories, together with names of editors, and in cases of national and regional newspapers, specialist correspondents. There are also lists of contacts on news and feature programmes at radio and TV stations. Also contains details of specialist freelance journalists in areas such as agriculture, computers, and medicine. Updated monthly. PIMS London plc is at Pims House, 4 St John's Place, St John's Square, London EC1M 4AH. PIMS also publishes many other media directories covering the UK, Europe and the US.

PR Planner

Two volumes, one for the UK, the other for Europe. Similar approach to *PIMS*, listing publications by category with names of editors and special correspondents. Radio and TV news and feature programmes also covered. *PR Planner* is at Media Publishing Ltd, Hale House, 290–6 Green Lane, London N13 5TP.

British Rate and Data (BRAD)

Mainly aimed at advertisers, but containing a brief description of most British publications arranged in categories. Also includes editors and circulations along with other key staff members. Updated monthly. *BRAD* is at Maclean Hunter Ltd, Maclean

Hunter House, Chalk Lane, Cockfosters Road, Barnet, Herts EN4 0BU.

Editors

Published in six volumes *Editors* provides comprehensive lists of journalists. Six volumes cover all publications in UK together with lists of special correspondents, and London correspondents of foreign press. *Editors* is at Editors (Media Directories) Ltd, 9–10 Great Sutton Street, London EC1V 0BX.

Willings Press Guide

Contains useful list of magazines and newspapers in Britain and overseas countries. Published annually. *Willings* is at Reed Information Services, Windsor Court, East Grinstead House, East Grinstead, West Sussex RH19 1XA.

Writers' and Artists' Yearbook

New edition published every year. Contains lists of newspapers and magazines with brief descriptions of contents. Also details of book publishers and TV and radio in Britain and other English-speaking countries. *Writers' and Artists' Yearbook* is at A & C Black (Publishers) Ltd, 35 Bedford Row, London WC1R 4JH.

Benn's Media Directory

Comes in two volumes – UK and overseas. UK volume lists newspapers and magazines, the former by town, the latter by subject. Overseas volume lists 32,000 publications in 197 countries. Published annually. *Benn's Media Directory* is at Benn's Business Information Services Ltd, PO Box 20, Sovereign Way, Tonbridge, Kent TN9 1RQ.

In each of your essential target media arenas you should draw up a shortlist of several priority publications. Then you need to get more information on each of your shortlisted publications before deciding on your final priorities. You can do this by studying each of your shortlisted publication's media packs – the promotional material issued by the publication's advertising department – and sample issues.

In the case of broadcast media, you need to study programme listings and view or listen to video or sound tapes of shortlisted programmes.

Ask yourself the following questions.

- Do the shortlisted media match the target audiences identified in Data Module 1?

- Will the media be interested in the kind of information my company has to provide? Is our message relevant to the media's content?

- Are the treatment and style of the publication likely to prove helpful in getting our message across to our end audience?

- Are the media accessible: will they want to hear my message and are they likely to use it? (Try to be completely objective about this.)

You need to answer a fairly confident 'yes' to each of those questions before you make any publication a priority target for proactive attention.

When you have completed the exercise – and this will take a little time – you need to draw up a list of your prime target publications and align them with your audiences.

- First, using Data Module 3, cross-reference those squares where an 'essential' target audience is matched by an 'essential' target media arena. (You can, of course, also cross-reference audiences of lesser priority, such as 'important', with target media of lesser priority if you feel the exercise is useful.)

- Second, select from the 'essential' target audiences listed in Data Module 3 your first priority. Enter its name on the 'first priority audience' page of Data Module 4.

- Third, review the 'essential' target media arenas listed under your first priority audience in Data Module 3. Take those 'essential' target media and list them in order of priority on the 'first priority audience' page of Data Module 4. (Space is given for three priority target media arenas, but you can add further priorities if you wish.)

- Fourth, repeat the process for your second and third priority audiences, ranking each audience in importance. (Again, space is given in Data Module 4 for three priority audiences, but you can add further priorities if you wish.) For each priority audience, repeat the ranking of your priority target media arenas in the same way as for your first priority audience.

- Fifth, study the results of your prioritizing exercise. Ask yourself these questions.
  Am I satisfied with these priorities?
  Do they seem right for the needs of our company at the moment?

If you are not satisfied, make amendments. If you *are* satisfied with the ranking for each audience and each target media arena within each audience, the next step is as follows.

- Sixthly, list in order of priority in each target media arena those specific publications or programmes which are your preferred choice.

When you have carried out this exercise sufficiently rigorously, you should have:

- **Ranked** each of your 'essential' (and, if you wish, 'important' and 'useful') target audiences in order of priority;

- **Identified** each of the most effective channels for communicating with those audiences.

You still need to select journalists on each preferred media, and that will be done after studying the next part of this section.

Remember ... choosing effective channels to reach key audiences is an essential ingredient in the success of a corporate communications campaign. It cannot be ignored.

DATA MODULE 4: TARGETING MEDIA ARENAS, PREFERRED MEDIA AND JOURNALISTS TO REACH TOP THREE PRIORITY AUDIENCES

FIRST PRIORITY AUDIENCE _____

Target media arena:	Preferred media:	Target journalists:

First priority:

_____

1 _____   1 _____
   2 _____

2 _____   1 _____
   2 _____

3 _____   1 _____
   2 _____

Second priority:

_____

1 _____   1 _____
   2 _____

2 _____   1 _____
   2 _____

3 _____   1 _____
   2 _____

Third priority:

_____

1 _____   1 _____
   2 _____

2 _____   1 _____
   2 _____

3 _____   1 _____
   2 _____

SECOND PRIORITY AUDIENCE _____

Target media arena:	Preferred media:	Target journalists:
First priority:		
_____	1 _____	1 _____
		2 _____
	2 _____	1 _____
		2 _____
	3 _____	1 _____
		2 _____
Second priority:		
_____	1 _____	1 _____
		2 _____
	2 _____	1 _____
		2 _____
	3 _____	1 _____
		2 _____
Third priority:		
_____	1 _____	1 _____
		2 _____
	2 _____	1 _____
		2 _____
	3 _____	1 _____
		2 _____

THIRD PRIORITY AUDIENCE _____

Target media arena:	Preferred media:	Target journalists:

First priority:

_____

1 _____ 1 _____
                   2 _____

2 _____ 1 _____
                   2 _____

3 _____ 1 _____
                   2 _____

Second priority:

_____

1 _____ 1 _____
                   2 _____

2 _____ 1 _____
                   2 _____

3 _____ 1 _____
                   2 _____

Third priority:

_____

1 _____ 1 _____
                   2 _____

2 _____ 1 _____
                   2 _____

3 _____ 1 _____
                   2 _____

You now have a clear idea of the priorities of your audiences and of the pathways to them. You have also identified carefully the publications and programmes that can help you reach them.

So far, everything has been defined in terms of audiences and media. It is now time to introduce the human dimension.

HOW TO MAKE THE HUMAN FACTOR WORK IN YOUR FAVOUR

The human factor is important in any aspect of business, but this is especially true of corporate communications. So it helps to find out which media people are going to be most interested in your messages.

You have already identified the target media which are the highest priorities in your proactive public relations campaign. Now you need to target those writers or broadcasters (or, in the case of radio and television, often researchers) who will be most interested in your message.

In many cases this means identifying the specialist correspondents that might want to write about your company. There are three main ways to do this.

- First, refer to the specialist publications and journalist directories mentioned in Checklist 2.2 on p. 53.

- Second, get copies of the publications on your preferred list. Study them carefully. See which journalists write about topics that might make them interested in your company.

- Third, call the publication or programme and ask. Speak to the editor on smaller publications. On larger publications, generally ask for the news editor or features editor. In the case of radio or television programmes talk to the producer, editor or a researcher.

Now, returning to Data Module 4, make a list of those journalists on your target publications that may be receptive to your message and who are your prime targets.

If you are interviewed by a journalist, it helps to know something about their special interests and the approach they take to writing about different subjects. Now that you have clearly identified your preferred publications and target journalists, you are in a position to get your PR staff to keep a cuttings file of the major pieces by your target journalists. By reading these you will develop a feel for the way the journalist writes about your industry and the kinds of subjects he or she is interested in.

Remember, journalists are people too and they identify with other people who seem to be on their wavelength. The human factor is as important between a journalist and the people he or she interviews as in any other business relationship. In fact, it is quite probably more important than in most. Like any other business relationship, it works best when there is mutual respect and trust.

Remember ... taking the trouble to understand a journalist's interests and approach will provide you with a significant edge in getting him or her interested in your message and will be helpful if you meet for an interview.

TO SUM UP

In this chapter you've:

- discovered that the starting post for your corporate communications campaign is a definition of the audiences you need to address;

- worked out a methodology for pinpointing the audiences you really need to reach;

- reviewed 15 possible target media arenas as channels for reaching your priority audiences;

- completed a detailed review of priority audiences, target media, preferred publications and programmes, and selected specific journalists;

- discovered that the human factor can be made to work in your favour.

Defining Your Corporate Personality

'You ask me what it is I do. Well actually, you know,
I'm partly a liaison man and partly PRO.'

John Betjeman '*Executive*'

In 'Defining Your Corporate Personality' you'll learn about:

○ what you need to know before you define your corporate personality;

○ how you can find out how outsiders view your company;

○ how you can make your corporate personality serve your business objectives;

○ the 13 components that help to form your corporate personality.

WHAT YOU NEED TO KNOW BEFORE YOU DEFINE YOUR CORPORATE PERSONALITY

Over the years, your company will have developed a 'personality' – some people prefer to call it an 'image'. It doesn't matter whether you've actively tried to promote that personality or whether it's just happened. Your company will still have one.

It is generally recognized that personality or image is an important ingredient in business success. Does your corporate personality do your company justice? A helpful personality paves the way for your company's products and services. And it helps in many other ways – for example, by making your company one that people trust, believe is socially responsible or want to work for.

A positive corporate personality is especially important in an age of predatory capital and hostile takeovers. Your corporate personality can prove a major asset whether you are attacking or defending in a takeover battle. For example, several chairpersons and/or chief executives have invested heavily in personal press coverage before embarking on an aggressive round of takeovers. The fact that journalists knew and understood their track records encouraged helpful press comment during the takeover battles. And they had an undoubted edge when up against more bureaucratic and less communicative companies.

An unhelpful personality hinders business success. It can undermine your efforts to market your products and services. And it can create suspicion or antagonism among people who could be helpful to you.

It is desirable that all managers have an understanding and an empathy for their company's personality. But it is especially important that you, as a spokesperson, have a clear understanding of the personality of your company. This means both the personality your company has now – and the personality you want to achieve in the future. In any event, you will find it very difficult to build an effective communications campaign that is helpful to and consistent with your company's mission, its aims and business objectives, if you do not fully understand what personality your company wants to project.

So, the first need is to understand the position you are in. Few companies are totally satisfied with their personality and their image in the media. Even if you *are* satisfied with the way your corporate personality is seen by outsiders, you will still want to promote and defend it. Whichever is the case with your company, as a spokesperson you need to be fully aware of how your company is seen. And of your company's mission, strategy and objectives.

> **Remember ...** what you want to achieve as a company spokesperson is to provide the media with messages that will help to create the corporate personality your company is seeking to build and support its mission, strategy and objectives.

In developing your corporate personality, you need to answer two key questions.

- What images do our key audiences already have of our company?

- What personality do we wish to portray to these audiences?

The first step in answering these questions is to find out how your company is currently seen by your key target audiences. How you do this will depend on six factors.

1. Who your audiences are

Different audiences may view your company in different ways. For example, your employees may take a different view to your customers.

2. How large your company is

This may influence the number of people who already have an image of your company. For example, a small company may project only a weak personality, even in its specialist niche markets, whereas almost everybody in the population will have some kind of image of a corporate giant like British Telecom or British Gas. Alternatively, a small company may have a focused image while a large conglomerate has a diffuse one.

3. How long your company has been established

A new company may begin with a 'clean slate'. A long-established company may have a history and reputation either to 'live down' or 'live up to'. For example, for a number of years, Rank Xerox has been working hard to position itself as a supplier of high quality office systems products and services. Yet because of its history and continuing market leadership, it is still often referred to in the media as a 'copier company'.

4. The nature of your market place

Your company's image may be affected by the type of market place you are in, and the activities and personalities of your competitors. For example, there are several reputable companies in the 'time share' business – one a division of a major international construction company. But because the market has a poor reputation for fair dealing and value for money, all the companies in it are tarred with the same brush.

5. Your customers

They may regard image as an important feature of your products and their own image will help to shape that of your company. The people who buy Gucci shoes, Rolls Royces, Fortnum and Mason hampers or Purdy shotguns help to create the image of the products they purchase.

6. The size of your planned corporate communications campaign

This is important because it will determine the resources put into the campaign – and into measuring its effectiveness. Resources, in turn, need to reflect the size of the job to be done.

HOW YOU CAN FIND OUT HOW OUTSIDERS VIEW YOUR COMPANY

An important first task is to get a clear idea of the image your company actually has, rather than the image you and your colleagues think it has. In order to get an accurate and objective view of the corporate personality your company is currently projecting, you need to assemble information about it. That information can come from a number of sources.

CHECKLIST 3.1: SOURCES OF INFORMATION ABOUT
     CORPORATE PERSONALITY

Market research

Tailor-made, structured surveys of carefully designated audiences are generally the most reliable form of data. But they can be expensive.

Customer surveys

These can often be conducted more cost-effectively using question-naires or telephone surveys. But they must be conducted objectively if they are to produce reliable results. They don't provide information about potential customers, but they help you find out what existing customers are thinking.*

Reports from sales staff

The sales team ought to be a source of regular useful feedback about how customers see your company. Encourage them to be objective in their assessments. You need to be told it 'as it is'.

Customer service departments

Their sharp-end role makes customer service departments a good source of information about how existing customers view your company. Encourage feedback, but remember that the views of a minority of customers may not be representative of the whole.

Staff surveys

Carried out in confidence and with mutual trust these can throw valuable light on how your company is seen by those closest to it.

Press cuttings

What the press is saying about your company – or not saying about it – will give you some idea of its personality (or lack of it).

Analysts' reports

What is written in stockbroker reports could influence share-holders and investors.

---

* The British Institute of Management report 'Beyond Quality' (1990), suggests customers should be viewed as partners or collaborators – part of your organization. That means encouraging open and frank feedback.

Of course, not all these sources will necessarily be relevant. But some of them will be. And there may be others unique to your organization that can be tapped for data.

From these data you should begin to assemble a picture of how the outside world views your company. You should try to be completely objective. In fact, you should seek to reduce the image that emerges to a written statement.

If it will help, think of your company in human terms and describe the personality it projects in terms of the following characteristics:

- age (is it youthful or old?);

- social background (is it upmarket or downmarket, aristocratic or middle class?);

- appearance (is it modern or traditional, smart or worn round the edges?);

- behaviour (is it friendly or stand-offish, helpful or unhelpful?); and

- attitudes (is it autocratic or approachable, caring or self-centred?).

When you have assembled and studied the information on your company's current personality try to describe the image your key audiences (identified in Chapter 2) have of you. Make it easier for yourself. Don't bother about writing sentences. Just use key words or phrases. And, if you wish, split the personality features into those that are helpful and those that are unhelpful. Fill in all this information in Data Module 5.

DATA MODULE 5: HOW KEY AUDIENCES VIEW YOUR COMPANY	Helpful image features	Unhelpful image features
First priority audience:		
Second priority audience:		
Third priority audience:		

(*NB:* Add details of more priority audiences if you wish.)

Having completed Data Module 5, you have identified strengths and weaknesses in your company's personality – as seen by the key audiences with which you need to communicate.

In particular you have:

- *highlighted* the fact that different key target audiences may each have their own particular image of your company;

- *identified* the helpful image features you already have with your key target audiences which will need to be built upon;

- *revealed* the unhelpful image features your company has with its key target audiences which will need to be rectified.

You are now in a better position to define the personality you wish to project. And to relate that personality to your company's mission, aims and objectives.

Remember ... to have a true understanding of your company's personality you need to be objective and critical and see it as others do. Without an objective understanding of your existing personality, it is not easy to determine ways in which it can be improved.

HOW YOU CAN MAKE YOUR CORPORATE PERSONALITY SERVE YOUR BUSINESS OBJECTIVES

You have now seen how your key target audiences currently view your company. You are now in a position to define the kind of corporate personality that you want to put across to those target audiences. When you have done that you will be able to start formulating the specific messages that will help to build that personality with your audiences.

But before you do that, you will need to make sure that your corporate personality reflects your company's mission and its business aims and objectives. The first step is to make sure that your company's mission has been clearly and explicitly defined. In many large companies this will already have been done. Some smaller and medium-sized companies, however, do not have a formal mission statement. If not, your company's most senior policy makers should spend the time needed to prepare a mission statement.

This mission statement not only makes it clear to everyone in the company where you are going, but it also helps you to describe your company's purpose to outsiders. Because of that, you need to get the mission statement right. So you can't afford to rush it. And you must make sure you and your colleagues are all working to the same mission statement.

Remember ... a mission statement describes your company's vision, role and purpose. It is essential if you wish to develop a corporate personality that serves your business needs.

CHECKLIST 3.2: FEATURES OF GOOD AND BAD MISSION STATEMENTS

The **good** mission statement is hard and specific about:

- the company's markets; and
- the benefits it offers.

And what is distinctive about:

- its approach to business;
- its products and services; and
- the qualities of its people.

It says things about your company that are:

- credible;
- memorable; and
- is a valuable guide to action.

The **bad** mission statement is:

- bland;
- too general;
- all things to all men;
- reads like a patched-up committee compromise;
- comes across as 'motherhood and apple pie';
- forgotten a moment later; and
- useless as a guide to action.

An unusual but interesting example of how important an effective mission statement can be is provided by the company Quicks, a commercial stationery supplier based in South London. The company is run by 'born again' Christians who seek to reflect their Christianity in the way their company operates. But it is illegal to discriminate against employees or potential employees on grounds of religion. The solution to the problem has been for the shareholders to adopt a mission statement that calls on the company and its staff to honour God in all they do, help people develop, pursue excellence and grow profitably. At the day-to-day management level, the company has adopted a non-denominational code of ethics which is compatible with the mission statement, but which does not offend against people of other religious beliefs, and provides a framework for effective management. The code requires employees to be courteous, to use clean speech, be truthful and of smart appearance. According to the code, employees must also respect confidentiality, make and keep realistic promises, and take care of company property.

Now complete Data Module 6 either with your existing or a new mission statement. Get the statement agreed by your company's senior management. Test it out on people both inside and outside your company. Refine it and redraft it until you have got it exactly right and it wins the support of your senior management team.

DATA MODULE 6:
YOUR COMPANY'S MISSION STATEMENT

Name of company: _____

Mission statement: _____

_____

_____

_____

_____

_____

_____

Date of adoption of mission statement: _____

Statement approved by: _____

Statement to be circulated to: _____

_____

_____

_____

The mission statement defines the broad purpose of your company. But it doesn't tell you how you're going to achieve that purpose. That is the job of your **business aims** and **objectives**.

Aims are broad directions – they point the way. Objectives are more concrete. They describe the particular points you want to reach – generally within specific timescales. Objectives are the milestones of business life. Your corporate communications campaign will generally be more effective if it seeks to support specific business objectives. But it should always have your corporate mission and aims in mind. You will need to understand your company's objectives quite clearly if you are going to be an effective spokesperson. They ought to be written into your company's business plan.

The next step as a company spokesperson is to assess whether those business objectives are being aided or hindered by the company's current perceived personality. This is the purpose of Data Module 7.

In the left-hand column of Data Module 7 list your company's main business objectives. (Space is given for four business objectives, but you can add others on additional sheets if you wish.) In the next two columns of the Data Module, list against each business objective any feature of your company's current personality that is helping or hindering in the achievement of your objectives.

You'll need to refer back to the personality audit you conducted in Data Module 5.

DATA MODULE 7: HOW YOUR CORPORATE PERSONALITY AIDS OR HINDERS BUSINESS OBJECTIVES	Helpful personality features	Unhelpful personality features
Business objective 1:		
Business objective 2:		
Business objective 3:		
Business objective 4:		

Having completed Data Module 7, you should ask yourself the following questions to check that you really have been rigorous and objective about assessing how your corporate personality impacts on business objectives.

- Have I got to the heart of the problem?

- Have I made full use of the information available?

- Am I really looking at the company as outsiders see it?

Can you honestly answer 'yes' to each of those questions? If so, you are ready to move on to the next stage. You are ready to set about correcting existing deficiencies and building a corporate personality as you would like it to be.

THE 13 COMPONENTS THAT HELP TO FORM YOUR CORPORATE PERSONALITY

You may have a clear mental vision of what your company's personality is or ought to be. But at the end of the day that personality has to be expressed in words, because that is the main way in which it will be communicated to other people.

On the whole, successful companies tend to have very clear personalities. They know that a personality that supports their business objectives is helpful in the market place.

Quite simply, people like to feel they 'know who they are dealing with'. And remember that behaviour, consciously or unconsciously, is shaped and influenced by images, values, feelings and prejudices. Often more so than by rational calculations.

As William Hazlitt said: 'Prejudice is the child of ignorance.'

You might feel that a corporate personality is rather an amorphous object to get hold of. Where do you start? How do you describe it in a meaningful way?

The best place to start is by looking at the elements that combine to give your company a personality. There are 13 main components that are worth examining, but you should recognize that the relative strength and importance of each of these components will vary depending on the company.

CHECKLIST 3.3:
COMPONENT PARTS OF CORPORATE PERSONALITY

The 13 components are:

1. mission;
2. history;
3. culture;
4. nationality;
5. location;
6. ownership;
7. structure;
8. people;
9. markets;
10. products and services;
11. technology;
12. competition;
13. strengths and weaknesses.

Mission

Your company's vision, its role and purpose.

History

Where your company has come from and what it's done in the past. For example, few companies can be more affected in personality terms by their history than British Rail. The age of the pre-war regional railway companies, nationalization, the history of strikes and various reorganizations – not to mention successive governments' policies on funding – have all left an indelible legacy on the corporation's corporate personality.

Culture

The philosophy, character and style that imbues your company's business life. Colourings, a company set up by Anita Roddick and

Barbara Daly to provide cosmetics for Body Shop, has a culture that merges business life with concern for broader issues. Each week, staff get a free half-hour when they can write letters to governments or organizations on issues they feel strongly about.

Nationality

Your country of origin, more than the countries where you operate. In its British publicity, car maker Audi stresses that it is German – to the extent of having a German sales slogan: *Vorsprung durch technik*. The reason: German cars have a reputation for quality.

Location

Where you are based. The personality of a geographical region can impact on your company. For example, financial institutions base themselves in the City of London; whisky makers in Scotland.

Ownership

The number and kind of people or institutions that own your company. When doing its initial market reseach, the team that set up *The Independent* newspaper found a lot of people didn't like newspapers whose policies seemed dominated by the prejudices of their proprietors. The solution: to give all the paper's 180 journalists shares in the enterprise and limit any one person or institution's holding to 15 per cent.

Structure

The way your business is organized and its internal reporting system and controls. When the late Harold Geneen ran ITT with an iron hand (and not much of the velvet glove), the tight centralized structure of the management said much about the kind of company it was. And, indeed, helped lead it into several damaging enterprises.

People

The kind of people who work for you and the style and approach they adopt to their work. The late Thomas Watson had a vision of an IBM 'company man'. IBM specializes in the 'white-shirt, blue-suit, dry-handshake' company salesperson.

Markets

Where you choose to do business, both geographically and by vertical sector.

Products and services

The type of products and services you offer, along with their quality, design, reliability, etc. Aware that auditing was increasingly being seen as a 'commodity' service, KPMG Peat Marwick McLintock commissioned a survey on the public's perceptions of auditors. According to Mike Steen, author of *Audits and Auditors: what the public thinks* (1989) based on the survey findings: 'Much has been, and continues to be, written by interested parties on the accounting and auditing professions. But to date there has been little evidence available to support the assumptions we make about the public and its views on these matters.'

Technology

In some cases a reputation for technology can go beyond individual products. Pilkington Glass, a pioneer of the flat glass process, retains and has recently sought to reinforce its reputation for technological excellence, independent of individual products.

Competition

The rivals you are up against and the way you fight your battles for market share. Car rental company Avis made great play in its corporate personality of being 'Number two' (second to Hertz) – and, therefore, having to try harder.

Strengths and weaknesses

What you think you're good at. What others think you're poor at.

It is quite useful to look on these components as the ingredients in a recipe. You need all the ingredients in order to give your cake the right flavour. But you'll use the ingredients in different weights and in different ways, depending on the kind of cake you're baking.

All of the above components can contribute to your corporate personality – or you may have a personality that is dominated by one or two of them. But it is an illuminating exercise to analyze the role each of them performs as a means of highlighting corporate personality strengths and weaknesses.

Now it is time for you to describe the image you wish to present to the outside world of each of these component parts in your own company. You can do this using Data Module 8. This is no simple task, but there are some ways to make it easier.

- **Force yourself to be brief.** That way you'll concentrate on essentials. Don't bother with sentences. Key words and phrases are what you're looking for.

- **Select words that express the precise shade of meaning you're aiming at.** Use a thesaurus to help.

- **Test each personality statement.** Ask yourself how it differentiates your company from its competitors.

- **Test each personality statement against your busi-**

ness objectives. Ask yourself whether it will help or hinder your business objectives.

- **Test each image statement against the current perceived images of your company.** See Data Module 5. Ask yourself whether they reinforce strengths and correct weaknesses.

- **Avoid 'motherhood' statements.** Such as 'being the best' or 'providing value for money'. Say precisely what makes you the best or provides value for money.

DATA MODULE 8: STATEMENTS ON COMPONENT PARTS OF YOUR CORPORATE PERSONALITY

Under each of the following headings describe in a few words or phrases the distinctive image that your company wants to portray. If you feel a particular heading is not important to your corporate personality, leave it blank.

Mission:

History:

Culture:

Nationality:

Location:

Ownership:

Structure:

People:

Markets:

Products and services:

Technology:

Competition:

Strengths and weaknesses:

You have now defined the raw ingredients of your corporate personality. The next step is to give weight to each of the ingredients mentioned in Data Module 8 and produce one succinct statement that neatly and precisely expresses how you want your company to be seen. This should be done using Data Module 9.

There are three techniques that may be helpful in producing a final corporate personality statement.

- First, looking at what you have written in Data Module 8, assess which are the most important image statements for your company.

- Secondly, search for common themes in the most important of your statements.

- Thirdly, look for key words and phrases that can help to light up your personality statement and make it distinctive.

DATA MODULE 9: A DESCRIPTION OF THE CORPORATE PERSONALITY YOUR COMPANY IS SEEKING TO ACHIEVE

Company: _____

Corporate personality statement: _____

_____

_____

_____

_____

_____

_____

Date corporate personality statement drafted: _____

Approved by: _____

Statement circulated to: _____

_____

_____

_____

_____

Now that you have prepared a corporate personality statement, you should test it against your company's mission statement in Data Module 6 and the business objectives described in Data Module 7. Then, ask yourself whether the company you have described in your personality statement is the kind of company that could achieve the mission and objectives it has set itself.

Also, test your personality statement against the audiences you have identified as priorities. Will the personality you have defined enhance your business prospects with these audiences? Specifically, does the corporate personality you have defined reinforce the helpful image features you have already identified and correct the unhelpful features?

If you answer 'No' to this question there is a deficiency in your personality statement. You need to go back and decide where you have failed to describe your desired personality adequately.

If you answer 'Yes' to this question you have an image statement that will be at the heart of the work you do as a company spokesperson. Make sure that anyone who is likely to meet the media is completely familiar with this image statement. And at every stage in the future, test what you are doing against whether it furthers the propagation and understanding of your desired corporate personality.

TO SUM UP

In this chapter you've:

- found out why a helpful corporate personality can assist your company to achieve business success;

- identified ways of finding information about how key audiences view your company;

- discovered how to assess the image key audiences have of your company and whether your corporate personality helps or hinders your company's business objectives;

- learned how, by focusing on the 13 main components of corporate personality, you can build a desired personality for your company that helps its business objectives and aligns with its corporate mission.

◄ 4 ►

Creating Your Messages

❝He that will write well in any tongue must follow this counsel of Aristotle to speak as the common people do, to think as wise men do; and so should every man understand him, and the judgement of wise men allow him.❞

Roger Ascham, 16th century writer and philosopher

In 'Creating Your Messages' you'll learn about:

- o why it is important to develop effective company messages;

- o why you need to understand the different characteristics that messages can have;

- o how to relate proactive messages to your business objectives;

- o how to relate your messages to your priority audiences;

- o how to identify and develop reactive messages that enhance your corporate personality;

- o how to build messages that grab the media's attention;

- o the key questions about your company that you'll be asked most often.

WHY IT IS IMPORTANT TO DEVELOP EFFECTIVE COMPANY MESSAGES

As a company spokesperson you are in the front line of putting your company's case to the media. If you are to do this effectively you will, as we have already seen, be closely involved in relating your company's corporate communications campaign to its mission, aims and objectives. But you will also need to play a significant role in developing the kinds of messages that are put to the media. And in putting those messages yourself in direct meetings with journalists.

Before we look at the detail of developing effective messages, it will be useful to answer two important questions.

1. What are company messages?

As far as the media are concerned, a message is any information that they get from your company. A well thought out and carefully drafted statement is a message. So are hasty and ill-conceived remarks gabbled to a journalist over a telephone between meetings. 'I haven't got time to talk to you,' is a message. 'No comment' is a message. It is all too easy for an ill-considered remark to become an important 'message' in the eyes of your target audience. James Callaghan seriously undermined his position as prime minister by his casual approach to the 'winter of discontent' troubles in 1978/9. His 'Crisis? What crisis?' comment was quoted more often than anything else he said. (Even though he didn't actually use those words.)

The lesson here is that if you want your company to be presented positively in the media, it needs to understand the importance of developing effective messages.

The key word here is *effective*. Many companies send out huge amounts of information to the media, but too little of it is effective communication. Like firing a blunderbuss, they spray out information indiscriminately. Some of it may score a hit, but much of it will be wasted. And some may even do unwanted damage because it was not properly targeted. Writer Keith Waterhouse has written: 'Ninety five per cent of the handouts that reach me as a *Daily Mail* columnist don't even reach the scrunching stage. They glide, unread and often unopened – you get to recognize the envelopes – straight from desk to bin.'

In seeking to reach everyone these companies reach no one. In wanting to say everything, they say nothing. They confuse rather than clarify. You need to make sure that this does not happen in your company.

Remember . . . as a spokesperson, you need to manage the communication process in your company, so that only effective messages are communicated to the media.

So, what is an effective message? All activity should have a purpose. An effective message does more than tell people what you're doing. It *shows* people what you're doing. And *why*. It is a message that promotes *understanding* to the audience at which it was aimed.

In promoting understanding, it helps to shape *attitudes*. And it is other people's attitudes – potential customers' to your products, neighbours' to your factory development plans, students' to their employment prospects with you, employees' to your restructuring plans – that play a vital role in helping or hindering in the achievement of your company's objectives.

Remember . . . an effective message does more than communicate information. It promotes understanding. By promoting understanding, it shapes attitudes to your company, its products and its activities.

And that brings us to the second question.

2. Why do we need company messages?

As we have seen, an effective message is more than just a collection of facts and figures, of information. It is designed to promote understanding, generally within a clearly defined audience of people.

This means that the information about anything you want to communicate – your company's annual results, the appointment of a new managing director, the launch of a new product – has to be structured and shaped to generate the understanding.

> **Remember ...** information by itself does not lead to understanding. Too much information, poorly structured information, badly targeted information can get in the way of understanding. According to David O'Brien, while managing director of Rank Xerox (UK): 'Too much information without the ability to assimilate, absorb, conclude and communicate, only serves to cause confusion. Information is only of value when it results in better understanding.'

Having said that, it doesn't mean the information you want to provide has to be distorted. Still less does it mean that it has to be artificially 'manufactured'. Indeed, if your message is less than the truth, if it fails to be an effective representation of what you are trying to achieve, it will not ring true.

By suggesting that you should be structuring and shaping your message, we mean presenting the information you have to provide in a way that promotes the understanding you are hoping to generate. Hence, shaping attitudes in the way you want.

Moreover, when messages have been created, it is important that all managers who are acting as spokespeople – and who may have some responsibility for communicating them to the media – know about and understand them. A typical reaction from a manager nominated to be a spokesperson and to meet the media is this: 'I know my company. I've been working for it for years. I'll have no difficulty talking about it and answering questions.' That casual approach to being a spokesperson usually ends in tears. Talking about your company to the media is not the same as chatting about it casually to friends in the pub.

Time after time, when managers fail to communicate what they want to say effectively or get into difficulty in interviews, it is because they have adopted that kind of casual approach and have not taken the time to prepare or understand their messages beforehand.

> **Remember ...** it is precisely because you are so close to your company, subjectively involved in its business and emotionally committed to its success, that you need to stand back and understand clearly those messages you want to put across to outside audiences.

When you meet journalists you are not being asked to talk generally about your company and its activities. You are being interviewed about a specific topic for an article with a focus that the journalist will create.

If you are clear in your own mind about the messages you want to convey – and about the implications of those messages for your company – you will be able to deploy them more persuasively to your interviewer and influence the focus of his or her article.

THE THREE KINDS OF MESSAGES YOU'LL NEED AS A SPOKESPERSON

As a company spokesperson, you will need messages to fit THREE sets of circumstances.

- **Proactive messages:** These are the messages that you want to convey about your own company and its products and services. They are the positive statements that will help to fulfil your corporate mission, achieve your business objectives and shape the public's perception of your company as you want it to be seen.

- **Reactive messages:** These are the messages that you will be asked to provide by the media in reaction to things such as developments in your industry or the views of public bodies, communities and other companies about your business. Some companies have Monday morning conferences so that they can identify possible 'reactive' issues for the week ahead. The *UK Press Gazette* publishes a weekly diary of forthcoming news events.

- **Crisis messages:** These are the messages that you will need to have ready in advance to deal with inevitable media interest in any major business reverse, mishap or disaster that may hit your company.

WHY YOU NEED TO UNDERSTAND THE DIFFERENT CHARACTERISTICS THAT MESSAGES CAN HAVE

You have seen that there are three kinds of messages that you may be called on to develop and deliver as a company spokesperson. Each of these types of messages – proactive, reactive, crisis – could have a number of features.

Before you start to draw up the specific messages for your company, you need to understand the different features that your message could have. If you are aware of these features, it will help you to understand more clearly the kind of message you are developing.

And by doing that, you will be able to shape the message more precisely, both to serve your company's own business objectives and to provide an effective communication through your targeted media to your ultimate audiences.

As a means of focusing attention it is useful to consider the message features in four pairs. It is not usual for an individual message to have both characteristics within each pair, although in some cases it can happen. But a company could easily have different messages which between them possess all the features.

1. **Strategic**

A message that is fundamental to your company's corporate mission.
Consider: Its impact on the different audiences it will reach.

or
Tactical

A message that aims to help you achieve a given business objective or objectives.
Consider: Whether it has been targeted precisely enough to the audiences it is intended to reach.

2. **Single**

A message that consists of just one central idea or theme.
Consider: Whether the message has been expressed with sufficient clarity to promote the understanding you seek.

or
Multiple

A message that consists of a cluster of ideas that interrelate to one another.
Consider: The danger of the media using only part of the message in the absence of the full context.

3. **Exclusive**

A message that is aimed just at the one audience you are concerned to reach.
Consider: The effect of the message reaching audiences other than those for which it is primarily intended.

or
Divisible

A message that can be divided into its component parts and targeted at different types of audience.
Consider: The effect of the message reaching audiences for which it was not primarily intended.

4. **Good news**   Positive information that you are anxious should reach the widest possible audience.
Consider: The danger of hype, making genuine good news seem 'too good to be true'.

or

Bad news   Negative or unhelpful information that you cannot avoid releasing to the media.
Consider: Ways of reducing the impact, including presenting the information in a positive context or blunting its effect by coupling it to an item of good news.

Examples of different message features

- **Strategic:** John Sculley, chairman and chief executive officer of Apple Computer Inc, is said to have been lured to the company from Pepsi Cola with the strategic question: 'Do you want to sell soft drinks or change the world?'

- **Multiple:** A budget speech by the Chancellor of the Exchequer is an example of a multiple message – with something for everyone. But chancellors, aware of the fact that multiple messages can appear to lack an overall theme, take care to provide one before they sit down. They will announce that theirs is a 'steady-as-she-goes' budget, a 'budget for growth', a 'budget for enterprise', etc.

- **Exclusive:** For example, a chairperson's report to staff is the kind of statement that he or she might not necessarily want to be communicated to customers, dealers or distributors.

- **Good news:** Make sure the good news is given prominence. One company, to be honoured with a visit by the Princess of Wales, sent out a long press release – and mentioned the visit in the last paragraph.

- **Bad news:** Machiavelli counselled that it is a good idea to let all the bad news out in one go. Dribble it out and you'll have a succession of negative stories instead of one bad headline.

HOW TO RELATE PROACTIVE MESSAGES TO YOUR BUSINESS OBJECTIVES

You now need to develop the specific proactive messages you are going to use to support your corporate mission and your business objectives. You also need to be sure that your messages are going to support the corporate image you want to portray. In some cases, this will mean changing your existing company image to one that is more helpful to your business objectives.

This is a good time to remind yourself of the *corporate mission* you have defined in Data Module 6. And of the *business objectives* listed in Data Module 7. You should also refresh your mind on the desired *corporate personality* you are seeking, by referring back to Data Modules 8 and 9. Finally, you need to remind yourself about the key *priority audiences* and *target media* for reaching them by looking again at Data Module 4.

The subject matter of your messages will depend on the audience you are addressing. So it is worth looking at each of your main priority audiences in turn to see what possible messages might be relevant. (Your possible audiences are listed in Data Module 1.)

The checklists that follow are not intended to be fully comprehensive. Indeed, in each category there could be dozens, if not hundreds of potential message areas. But they do show the kinds of areas that you might look at for suitable messages for given audiences.

CHECKLIST 4.1: POSSIBLE MESSAGE AREAS FOR PRODUCTION AUDIENCES

1. Management

- Company results
- Management changes and appointments
- Acquisitions and divestments
- Mergers and joint ventures
- New orders
- New investment

2. Staff

- Company results
- Management changes
- Changes in working practices
- Opening and closing of offices and plants
- New remuneration plans

3. Sales team

- New products
- Sales successes
- Bonuses, awards and incentives

4. Suppliers

- New manufacturing processes
- Quality procedures and requirements

5. Dealers/Distributors

- New products
- Product changes
- Sales incentives

6. Retailers

- Product changes
- Packaging changes
- Price and discount arrangements
- Advertising and other promotional campaigns

CHECKLIST 4.2: POSSIBLE MESSAGE AREAS FOR END-USER AUDIENCES

8. Existing customers

- Product strategy
- New products
- Case studies
- Price changes and options
- Benefits derived by users

9. Potential customers

- Product strategy
- Understanding of end-user needs
- Case studies
- Benefits derived by users

10. Rivals' customers

- Product strategy
- New business wins
- Competitive strengths

11. Non-users

- Competitive strengths
- Product strategy
- Benefits derived by existing users

CHECKLIST 4.3: POSSIBLE MESSAGE AREAS FOR INFLUENCER AUDIENCES

13. Local communities

- Employment prospects
- Participation in community life
- Financial contribution to community
- Care for environment

14. Government/public bodies

- Contribution to economy
- Role in technological innovation
- Size of exports

15. Elected officials

- Need for favourable financial treatment
- Need to promote internationally 'fair' trade
- Special problems needing help of government, etc

16. Investors

- Company results
- New strategy
- Acquisitions, mergers, joint ventures
- Major management changes

17. Special interest groups

- Product safety

- Environmental care

- Equal opportunities

- Education and training

18. Educational institutions

- Contribution to investment and training

- Employment prospects

- Career success stories

- Collaborative ventures with educational/research bodies

HOW TO RELATE YOUR MESSAGES TO YOUR PRIORITY AUDIENCES

As you can see, there is a huge number of possible messages for target audiences and a vast number of possible combinations of messages and audiences. You need to prioritize. You need to select the possible messages that will:

- most effectively reach your priority audiences; and

- help you to achieve your specific business objectives.

You can do this with the aid of Data Module 10 on p 107. In the column headed 'Possible messages' list those subjects that could be used. Be specific, not vague. As you want to gain immediate practical benefit from this exercise you should look for subjects that you could use during the next six months. List items such as specific product launches, company acquisitions, new business plans, etc.

Now, by adopting the methodology described, test each

possible subject against how effective it is likely to be in developing understanding of your company with your specific priority audiences and, thus, proving helpful in achieving business objectives.

1. Mark each of your potential messages using Column 1 against how effective it could be in achieving your company's business objectives. (Score 5 points for Very Effective, 4 points for Quite Effective, 3 points for Useful, 2 points for Worthwhile, 1 point for Ineffective.)

2. Mark each of your potential messages using Column 2 against the extent to which it is likely to promote understanding of your corporate personality with the relevant priority audience and thus shape attitudes which will be helpful in achieving your business objectives. (Score 5 points for Very Considerably, 4 points for Significantly, 3 points for A Little, 2 points for Very Little, 1 point for Not At All.)

3. Bearing in mind the ways in which you have identified your target media, mark each of your potential messages using Column 3 against how interesting it is likely to be to your target media. (Score 5 points for Very Interesting, 4 points for Fairly Interesting, 3 points for Of Some Interest, 2 points for Of Little Interest, 1 point for Of No Interest.)

Try to be as objective as possible when marking up Column 3. If you have external PR consultants, involve them in the exercise as they will bring knowledge of the real interests of the target media to the marking exercise.

4. Using Column 4 total up the marks for each item. You will now be in a position to see which messages ought to receive your priority attention in the immediate future.

Space has been provided for three priority audiences, but you can add pages for more priority audiences if you wish.

DATA MODULE 10: PRIORITIZING THE EFFECTIVENESS OF POSSIBLE MESSAGES FOR PRIORITY AUDIENCES

Priority audience 1 _____

Possible messages	Column 1	Column 2	Column 3	Total
1.	[ ]	[ ]	[ ]	[ ]
2.	[ ]	[ ]	[ ]	[ ]
3.	[ ]	[ ]	[ ]	[ ]
4.	[ ]	[ ]	[ ]	[ ]
5.	[ ]	[ ]	[ ]	[ ]

(*NB:* You can continue with as many possible messages as you wish on continuation sheets.)

Priority audience 2_____

Possible messages	Column 1	Column 2	Column 3	Total
1.	[ ]	[ ]	[ ]	[ ]
2.	[ ]	[ ]	[ ]	[ ]
3.	[ ]	[ ]	[ ]	[ ]
4.	[ ]	[ ]	[ ]	[ ]
5.	[ ]	[ ]	[ ]	[ ]

(*NB:* You can continue with as many possible messages as you wish on continuation sheets.)

Priority audience 3_____

Possible messages	Column 1	Column 2	Column 3	Total
1.	[ ]	[ ]	[ ]	[ ]
2.	[ ]	[ ]	[ ]	[ ]
3.	[ ]	[ ]	[ ]	[ ]
4.	[ ]	[ ]	[ ]	[ ]
5.	[ ]	[ ]	[ ]	[ ]

(*NB:* You can continue with as many possible messages as you wish on continuation sheets.)

Now, extract the information from Data Module 10 and list in Data Module 11 the key messages which will have proactive priority in the next few months.

DATA MODULE 11: YOUR COMPANY'S PRIORITY MESSAGES FOR THE NEXT SIX MONTHS

Priority audience 1 _____

   Messages 1. _____

                2. _____

                3. _____

                4. _____

Priority audience 2 _____

   Messages 1. _____

                2. _____

                3. _____

                4. _____

Priority audience 3 _____

   Messages 1. _____

                2. _____

                3. _____

                4. _____

By going through the admittedly rigorous task of listing, defining and prioritizing the messages you could disseminate over the next few months, you will have effectively drawn up an *agenda for action*. Moreover, you will have created a situation in which the information you do disseminate to the media should both serve your immediate business objectives and create better understanding of your company and its activities among your priority audiences.

But, just as your immediate business objectives change rapidly within the overall framework of your corporate mission and aims, so will your specific messages. For this reason, the process of message identification and prioritization needs to be repeated regularly.

Remember ... in any dynamic business, specific messages will change quite rapidly. For that reason, this exercise ought to be undertaken at least twice a year and form the basis of the company's priority messages for the following six months.

HOW TO IDENTIFY AND DEVELOP REACTIVE MESSAGES THAT ENHANCE YOUR CORPORATE PERSONALITY

John Donne said 'No man is an island'. Well, neither is a company. It carries on its business in an environment that is influenced by the government and public bodies, other businesses, its local community and many other special interest groups.

This means that as a company spokesperson you will sometimes be called on to comment on events that are taking place in the wider business world. You might consider this an unwelcome interruption to your daily business life or you might think that it obscures the main thrust of your proactive media effort.

In fact, if you do the following three things, you can make your reactive messages as effective in serving your corporate mission and business objectives as your proactive messages. These three things are:

- anticipate;
- plan;
- respond.

Let's look at each of these in turn.

1. Anticipate

Many companies now carry out issue monitoring and management exercises. Different operating units are asked to identify and prioritize external developments in the business environment, assess their likely impact on the company and suggest what action the company needs to take in response.

With careful and intelligent thought you can identify those areas where you could be called on to provide a reactive message. Often that message would be as a result of something that a third party has done or is planning to do. Those third parties include the following groups.

CHECKLIST 4.4: THIRD PARTIES THAT COULD IMPACT ON YOUR COMPANY

Government

- Which policies are likely to impact on your business?

Parliament

- Which new laws could impact on your business?

Local councils/communities

- Which local authorities could impact on your business?

■ Which local pressure groups/individuals?

European Community

■ Which legislation and Directives could impact on your business?

Foreign governments

■ Does your company do business in other countries whose governments could have an impact on it?

Competitive businesses

■ How could their plans impact your own business?

Collaborative businesses

■ With which firms are you involved in joint ventures?

Industry regulatory bodies

■ How will their rules and regulations impact on your business?

Industry associations

■ How will their policies and view of your industry affect your business?

Special interest groups

■ How will the policies and activities of pressure groups impact on your business?

Customers

■ How will the actions of important or high-profile customers affect your business?

Investors

■ What actions of which major investors could impact on your business?

■ Could you be a takeover target?

■ From whom?

Trade unions

■ Which unions are active or could be active in your company?

Suppliers

■ Which companies supply your business with important goods, materials or components?

Distributors/Dealers/Retailers

■ Which companies distributing or selling your products could have a measurable impact on your business?

Examples of the impact of third parties

● **Government:** Those corporations being prepared for privatization have to monitor a huge mass of material that is likely to have an impact on their financial performance and the service they provide to customers.

- **Competitive businesses:** Rupert Murdoch's News International must have been concerned by an amendment to the Broadcasting Bill, drawn up by (what was) British Satellite Broadcasting, that would subject overseas-based satellite broadcasters to the same regulations as British broadcasters.

- **Collaborative businesses:** Collaboration is likely to become more important for many companies. A survey by the Manchester-based Centre for Exploitation of Science and Technology showed many companies recognize that technology is an important factor in gaining competitive advantage. At the same time, many realize that they will need to enter collaborative agreements to access the technology they need cost-effectively.

- **Industry regulatory bodies:** Rules drawn up by regulatory bodies on the subject of commission disclosure are a major issue for insurance companies.

- **Special interest groups:** According to a survey conducted in 1990 by the Confederation of British Industry, few companies have a formal written policy concerning environmental issues, increasingly an important topic concerning special interest groups. PA Consulting Group, which conducted the survey, said that among those companies that did have an environmental policy, the main issues were air pollution, hazardous chemicals, river pollution, solid waste and water supply.

- **Investors:** Richard Koch of Strategy Ventures and Adrian Blackshaw of Blackwood have drawn up a list of the one hundred most vulnerable-to-takeover companies in the UK. Of the top 25, 16 appear in the FT-SE 100 Share Index. Koch and Blackshaw have also devised a 'vulnerability index' to assess a company's danger of being taken over. (The Strategy Ventures survey is available from 19 Buckingham Street, London WC2N. Tel: 071-839 6033.)

Taking the different kinds of bodies and groups in Checklist 4.4, use Data Module 12 to list those specific bodies that are likely to have a significant impact on your business.

Be specific as you do this. For example, don't just write down 'government', but list the government departments or bodies that will specifically impact on your business. After you have made the list you are going to give a weighting to the likely impact such organizations could have. The way to do this will be explained after Data Module 12.

DATA MODULE 12: THIRD PARTIES THAT INFLUENCE THE
BUSINESS CLIMATE IN WHICH YOUR COMPANY OPERATES

Third party group	Column 1	Column 2	Column 3	Total
Government:	[ ]	[ ]	[ ]	[ ]
Parliament:	[ ]	[ ]	[ ]	[ ]
Local councils/ Communities:	[ ]	[ ]	[ ]	[ ]
European Community:	[ ]	[ ]	[ ]	[ ]
Foreign governments:	[ ]	[ ]	[ ]	[ ]
Competitive businesses:	[ ]	[ ]	[ ]	[ ]
Collaborative businesses:	[ ]	[ ]	[ ]	[ ]
Industry regulatory bodies:	[ ]	[ ]	[ ]	[ ]
Industry associations:	[ ]	[ ]	[ ]	[ ]
Special interest groups:	[ ]	[ ]	[ ]	[ ]
Customers:	[ ]	[ ]	[ ]	[ ]
Investors:	[ ]	[ ]	[ ]	[ ]
Trade unions:	[ ]	[ ]	[ ]	[ ]
Suppliers:	[ ]	[ ]	[ ]	[ ]
Distributors/Dealers/ Retailers:	[ ]	[ ]	[ ]	[ ]

Just because a third party *can* have an influence on your business doesn't mean that it necessarily will do. And even if it does, that doesn't mean you will be called on to provide a reactive message. That depends on other factors.

You now need to weight these factors against the third parties identified in Data Module 12 in order to get an objective idea of those areas where you could be called on to make reactive comments. Mark Factor 1 in Column 1 and so on.

- First, in Column 1, is the impact sufficiently large to be of real importance to your business?
  (Score 5 points for Very Large, 4 points for Fairly Large, 3 points for Medium, 2 points for Fairly Small, 1 point for Very Small.)

- Secondly, in Column 2, are you the only company affected, or how do you rank among other companies similarly affected?
  (Score 5 points for Only Company Affected, 4 points for Main Company Affected, 3 Points for Affected Similarly to Comparable Companies, 2 points for Affected Less than Other Companies, 1 point for Affected Much Less than Other Companies.)

- Thirdly, in Column 3, does the media see your company as a source of valid and authoritative comment?
  (Score 5 points for Usually Seen, 4 points for Often Seen, 3 points for Occasionally Seen, 2 points for Not Often Seen, 1 point for Never Seen.)

- Fourthly, add up the separate points for each third party and enter in the Total Column. The highest points should indicate those third parties whose activities could result in your company having to provide reactive messages.

Now you need to relate the third parties that could trigger a need for a reactive message to your priority audiences. This will give you a correlation between the audiences you are seeking to reach and the possible reactive messages you might have to provide. You can do this in Data Module 13 below.

When you have completed this exercise, you may find that there are only a limited number of high-ranking third parties likely to trigger the need for reactive messages. Given that this is a time-consuming exercise, you will be wise to limit yourself to those that are of the highest priority. So, against each third party body mark whether or not you propose to take further action to pursue it.

DATA MODULE 13: NEED FOR POSSIBLE REACTIVE MESSAGES ANALYZED BY PRIORITY AUDIENCES

Priority audience 1 _____

Third parties that could trigger need for reactive messages:

1. _____ Points _____ Action/No action

2. _____ Points _____ Action/No action

3. _____ Points _____ Action/No action

Priority audience 2 _____

Third parties that could trigger need for reactive messages:

1. _____ Points _____ Action/No action

2. _____ Points _____ Action/No action

3. _____ Points _____ Action/No action

Priority audience 3 _____

Third parties that could trigger need for reactive messages:

1. _____ Points _____ Action/No action

2. _____ Points _____ Action/No action

3. _____ Points _____ Action/No action

2. Plan

You have now identified those areas in which you could be called on to deliver reactive messages. Next you need to plan to be informed about the relevant activities of those bodies you have marked for action in Data Module 13.

You must make sure that relevant activities of those third parties are monitored within your company. That is potentially a large task – and for a Times 100 company it will be a huge task. But for smaller to medium-sized companies the job can be kept manageable by concentrating only on the priority areas you have identified.

Companies that are members of the British Institute of Management, Institute of Directors, Confederation of British Industry or a chamber of commerce or trade association, should examine what information services they provide. Individual managers should check out what information services are offered by professional bodies to which they belong.

CHECKLIST 4.5:
SOURCES OF INFORMATION ABOUT THIRD PARTIES

Such sources of information about the third parties, whose activities you may need to monitor, include:

- Government Reports;
- Parliamentary Reports;
- European Commission Reports;
- European Parliament Reports;
- embassy circulars from relevant overseas countries;
- minutes of public bodies;
- other companies' annual reports;
- press cuttings;
- press releases from relevant third parties;
- reports from special interest groups;
- independent surveys;
- market research;
- analysts' reports;
- reports from industry associations;
- reports from regulatory bodies.

The above checklist cannot hope to include every type of material that you could possibly want to monitor. But it will give you some ideas on where to search for it.

You will need to make arrangements to receive material that is likely to be relevant to your business regularly. Then you need to set up a system to ensure the material is reviewed regularly and that all spokespeople are informed about information which bears on areas where they may need to develop reactive messages.

List in Data Module 14 the specific information that you need regularly.

DATA MODULE 14: SPECIFIC INFORMATION NEEDED FROM THIRD PARTY BODIES:

Government:

Parliament:

Local councils:

European Community:

Foreign governments:

Competitive businesses:

Collaborative businesses:

Industry regulatory bodies:

Industry associations:

Special interest groups:

Customers:

Investors:

Trade unions:

Suppliers:

Distributors/Dealers/Retailers:

Depending on your other responsibilities in your company, you may choose to review the material yourself. Alternatively, you may choose to have it reviewed by someone else – a public relations or public affairs adviser, for instance – who will prepare a report drawing your attention to key issues.

If you implement this system there is no guarantee that you will never be caught out. But it will ensure that you:

- develop a much deeper knowledge about how your company is affected by the world around it; and

- enhance your role as a spokesperson by becoming more knowledgeable about specific issues of importance to your company.

Remember . . . the object of planning is to make sure that you are already informed and have had time to consider your response when called on to provide a message about an external event.

---

3. Respond

You have identified priority areas in which you may be called on to deliver a reactive message. You have taken steps to keep yourself informed about them. Now how should you prepare yourself for possible approaches from the media?

You need to be prepared with reactive messages that:

- demonstrate to the media that you are knowledgeable and authoritative about the issues raised;

- have something distinctive and worthwhile to say about these issues;

- serve your company's business objectives by enhancing the company's corporate personality with priority audiences.

In most cases, if you have anticipated intelligently and armed yourself with relevant information, it is not difficult to make a reasonable assessment of what questions you could be asked.

It is worth noting that you don't have to wait for the worst to happen. One company anticipated the publication of a critical report by announcing a new safety procedure the day before. Being proactive, it seized the initiative and avoided some criticism.

Make sure that you develop possible responses when an issue arises which could result in a need for reactive comments. Then ask the following questions.

- Has our message been checked against the message features described at the start of this chapter?

- Does the message say something distinctive and worthwhile?

- Is the message credible?

- Are the facts supporting it completely accurate?

- Does the message support our company's business objectives?

- Which media are likely to want a comment on this issue?

- Is our message likely to be of relevance to their special concerns?

- Have we identified any likely supplementary questions?

Finally, you need to consider whether in fact this is an issue of sufficient importance to your company that it should become a proactive message. In other words, perhaps you shouldn't wait to be asked before communicating your views.

Remember ... if you think there is a likelihood of your being asked to provide a comment about a developing issue or event, do not wait until you are asked. Prepare in advance – and you will be more effective.

Crisis messages

There are many special factors affecting crisis messages, and these will be fully dealt with separately in Chapter 8.

HOW TO BUILD MESSAGES THAT GRAB THE MEDIA'S ATTENTION

So far you have identified what your messages should be about. Now you need to build and focus those messages so that they will be effective when you meet the media.

What are the features or characteristics of a desirable message?

CHECKLIST 4.6:
FEATURES OF DESIRABLE CORPORATE MESSAGES

A message should be:

Short
Media people are busy. They don't have time to waste while you get to the point.*

Simple
A good message is easy to grasp – even by someone who is not an expert in your company's areas of activity.

Specific
Don't be vague. Make it clear what your message is about.

Focused
The message should be developed with its ultimate audience clearly in mind.

* An important message doesn't have to be a long message. For example, the Lord's Prayer contains only 56 words, the 23rd Psalm 118, the Hippocratic Oath 217, the Gettysburg Address 266, and the 10 Commandments 297. Trivial messages can be long. The US Government Report on Cabbage Prices contains 26,911 words.

Tailored
It should also be crafted to meet the needs of the particular journalist or journalists who will be receiving it.

Positive
In the words of the song, accentuate the positive, eliminate the negative.

Accurate
A good message gets it right. Quality control should be applied to press material. The motto 'get it right first time' should be your watchword.

Authoritative
It has the ring of credibility because it comes from a spokesperson who has the authority to speak and who is in complete command of the subject.

Appropriate
It's the right message in the right place at the right time.**

Jargon free
Don't make it sound as if your message is in code.

Distinctive
Make sure your message is different. It should 'add value' to the topic under consideration.

As you draw up your messages, test them against the criteria in Checklist 4.6. A message can usually be improved. The key tests in the checklist can help to focus on any areas of weakness in your message so that you can correct them.

If your message has all the qualities listed in the checklist, it is

** The Frontline Initiative, which seeks to tap skills in the North to solve shortages in the South, found that it had the right message in the right place when it managed to get an article in the *Sunday Telegraph*. Chief executive Horace Mitchell said: 'Timing is everything. Since the article, my telephone hasn't stopped ringing.'

well on its way to being the kind of message that will penetrate your target media.

Yet it is true that a message could have all those qualities and still lack the two essential ingredients to make journalists sit up and take notice. Ask yourself whether it is:

- newsworthy; and

- interesting?

In other words, does it pass a key test that journalists often use when deciding whether or not to publish a certain item of information? This is *the so-what? test*.

If the media failed to carry your message would their readers or viewers be any the poorer? Would they have been deprived of an important or useful piece of information?

In the words of Samuel Johnson: 'The two most engaging powers of an author are to make new things familiar and familiar things new.'

When you have drafted a message or piece of information for the media, it is useful to submit it to rigorous questioning.

First

- Have you really focused sharply enough on your audience?

- Have you identified with their needs?

- Do you understand their problems and point of view?

- Is your message really tuned into what they want to know?

Second

- Is your message as simple as you can make it without distorting the meaning?

- Are you sure you can't refine it further?*

- Have you really got to the heart of what you want to say?

* As George Bernard Shaw once wrote to a friend: 'I'm sorry it's such a long letter. I didn't have time to write a short one.'

Third

- Does your message touch on newsworthy themes in your business or industry area?
- Is your message plugged into the broader business world?
- Have you shown an appreciation of the wider context in which you are making your message?

Fourth

- Are you presenting your message clearly?
- Are you sure other people, without your special knowledge, can really understand it?
- From the way you have presented it, will they derive from it the lessons you want them to?

Fifth

- Have you pitched your message at the right level?
- Are you sure you're not talking down to your audience?
- At the same time are you certain you're not blinding them with science?

Sixth

- Is your message supported with convincing facts, examples, case studies and other evidence?
- Does the supporting evidence effectively reinforce your message?
- In fact, is there a sufficient weight of supporting evidence to make your case convincing?

Seventh

- Have you expressed your message as memorably as you can?

- Have you chosen your words carefully so that you light up rather than obscure your meaning?

- Have you avoided jargon and bureaucratic waffle?

Remember . . . try to construct your message in such a way that it meets the criteria of the checklist, but at the same time fulfils the tests needed to make it pass the So-What? test.

THE KEY QUESTIONS ABOUT YOUR COMPANY THAT YOU'LL BE ASKED MOST OFTEN

As a company spokesperson, you'll be speaking to the media about a wide range of your company's activities. The focus of individual messages you are called on to give will change from time to time, but there are certain questions you'll be asked time and time again. Although these questions are not hard to foresee, it is surprising how many spokespeople are unable to answer them convincingly.

The first area that you need to prepare information on is what can generally be called your company's *trading data*. It covers the basic facts and figures about your company's operation. Use Data Module 15 to complete this information.

DATA MODULE 15: YOUR COMPANY'S BASIC TRADING DATA

Company name: _____

Head office: _____

Other locations (with nature of facility): _____
_____

Subsidiaries/Divisions (with outline activities): _____
_____
_____
_____

Chief products and services: _____
_____
_____
_____

Year of founding: _____ Number of employees: _____

Turnover in last FY: _____ Profit/Loss in last FY: _____

Chairperson (with brief biographical details):_____
_____
_____
_____

Managing director/CEO (with brief biographical details):
_____
_____
_____

Other key managers: _____
_____

The second area where, as a company spokesperson, you need to be able to talk convincingly is on your *corporate personality*. As a spokesperson, you are setting out to be more than a provider of information. You are trying to create understanding.

Therefore, you need to have a thorough understanding of all the elements that go to make up your corporate personality. But more than that, you need to be able to talk about them convincingly and – for the listener – memorably.

That means you need to be able to describe each of the elements of your corporate personality in not more than three or four sentences. Those sentences ought to contain all the information the listener needs to understand the point you want to make.

The starting point in developing these corporate personality messages is to refer to the notes you made about your corporate personality back in Data Module 8 in Chapter 4.

Remember ... whatever the actual subject matter of specific messages, you will constantly return to central issues about your company's corporate personality. These need to be woven skilfully into all your messages in order to build the image and understanding you are seeking to achieve.

The notes in Checklist 4.7 on p 134 are designed to help you focus on some of the issues you need to address when developing your key company messages about corporate personality. You should write down your messages in Data Module 16.

Involve your colleagues in this exercise. Test your messages on senior people inside your company and on outsiders and involve your public relations and public affairs advisers.

CHECKLIST 4.7:
SOME QUESTIONS TO ASK WHEN DEVELOPING
CORPORATE PERSONALITY MESSAGES

Mission

- What is your company's mission?
- What is its purpose as a company?

History

- When was your company founded?
- What have been the significant milestones in its progress?

Culture

- What is your company's style?
- What is its philosophy of business?

Nationality

- In which country did your company have its origins?
- Does it want to be known as a national or international company?

Location

- How important is the location in underlining the company's skills and expertise?

Ownership

- Who owns your company?
- Which stock exchanges is it listed on?
- What is its market value and share price today?
- What were its highs and lows in the last year?

Structure

- How is your company organized?

- How does that structure contribute to its effectiveness?

People

- Who are the main people in your company?

- What do they bring to the business?

Markets

- Which markets is your company aiming at?

- How is it being effective in those markets?

Products and services

- What kinds of businesses are you in?

- What is the main focus of your products and services?

Technology

- Do you have a reputation for technology that goes beyond individual products?

- What part does it play in the company's success?

Competition

- Who are your main competitors?

- And why are you more than a match for them?

Strengths and weaknesses

- What are your company's strengths?

- And what have you to say about other people's claims about your perceived weaknesses?

DATA MODULE 16: MESSAGES ABOUT YOUR COMPANY'S CORPORATE PERSONALITY

Mission:

History:

Culture:

Nationality:

Location:

Ownership:

Structure:

People:

Markets:

Products and services:

Technology:

Competition:

Strengths and weaknesses:

TO SUM UP

In this chapter you've:

- found out why your company needs clear messages and learned about the differences between proactive, reactive and crisis messages;

- learned about the different features that shape the kinds of messages you produce;

- found out how to relate proactive messages to your company's business objectives;

- discovered how to identify and develop reactive messages that enhance your corporate personality;

- found out how to build messages that grab the media's attention;

- reviewed the key questions about your company that you'll be asked most often;

- developed message statements about the key elements of your corporate personality.

◀ 5 ▶

Preparing To Meet The Media

‘Much as journalists value the money they earn at their work, they – like Mafia hit men, the better type of hooker and Evel Knievel – could probably be persuaded to do it for nothing.’

Anthony Delano, journalist, in *Slip-Up*

In 'Preparing to Meet the Media' you'll learn about:

o what you need to know before you face a journalist;

o the nine main situations in which you will face the media.

WHAT YOU NEED TO KNOW BEFORE YOU FACE A JOURNALIST

Before you face a journalist, there are a few important things that you should know. It pays to take the time to find out about them – if necessary with the help of your public relations advisers.

The things you need to know about fall into three main categories:

1. your interviewer;

2. the purpose of the interview;

3. your company and message.

We'll now examine each of those areas in more detail.

1. What you should know about your interviewer

As with any business meeting, it pays to know something about the person or people you'll be meeting before you do so. It makes breaking the ice a little less painful when you do meet. It helps you to tune on to their wavelength more quickly. And, if we are honest, it gives you a psychological boost to know you've got 'something' on them.

Of course, it is not always practicable to find out much – or, indeed, anything – about the journalists you'll be meeting. At a press conference with 50 newshounds, you can't know all their names, let alone their life histories.

But there are certain circumstances when you really must take the time to brief yourself. These are:

- when you're facing a one-to-one interview;

- when you're holding a small briefing for a handful (say not more than four or five) journalists;

- when you're going on a facility trip (an organized visit for journalists) with a similarly small group of journalists;

- when there is a handful of journalists who cover your

141

industry or company and you're likely to meet them regularly at industry events or receive out-of-the-blue telephone calls from them for comments and quotes.

Your public relations professionals should be able to help with the spadework of finding out about these journalists. Get them to base it on the pro forma contained in Data Module 17.

DATA MODULE 17:
WHAT YOU NEED TO KNOW ABOUT KEY JOURNALISTS

- What is his/her correct Christian name and surname?
  (Are they spelt correctly? How do you pronounce them if tricky?)

- Which publication?
  (Have you seen a copy?)

- What position/job title does he or she hold?
  (Is your information up to date? Have you missed a promotion?)

- Likely knowledge/experience of your business/industry area?
  (A lot of background knowledge? Or will you need to get back to basics?)

- Any known special interests/hobby horses?
  (If so, do they support or conflict with your company's objectives and messages?)

- Any previous contact with your company?
  (What do they already know about the company?)

- Has he or she previously written about your company?
  (Was it sympathetic? Hostile? Purely factual?)

2. What you should know about the purpose of the interview

In some cases, you will have initiated the interview – it will be a proactive interview – but in others the request for the interview may come from the journalist. In these cases, it is essential to find out from the journalist what the purpose and focus of the interview will be.

There could be a number of different reasons why a journalist wants to interview you. Some of these are listed in Checklist 5.1.

CHECKLIST 5.1:
REASONS WHY JOURNALISTS WANT INTERVIEWS

- **To pursue a specific hard news story or feature article.** The focus is clear. It is about a specific product or project with which your company is involved, or about some corporate development in the company itself.

- **To increase general understanding.** The focus is fuzzy. It is about building background knowledge of your company or business area.

- **To obtain an example for a planned feature.** The focus is specific. It is about finding relevant examples for a specific article.

- **To seek information for a specific topic article.** The focus is clear but broad. The journalist may want 'educating' on a topic about which he or she knows little.

- **To seek evidence to support a point of view.** The focus is clear. But may be unhelpful if you do not subscribe to the point of view the journalist will pursue in his or her article.

- **To obtain information on customers or clients.** The true focus of the interview may be hidden. The journalist may not be primarily seeking information about your company, but about a customer in which he or she is particularly interested.

In practically all cases, a journalist will be prepared to reveal the purpose of the interview in advance. Indeed you should beware if he or she is not prepared to do so.

In the following examples the company gave out information which was useful for the journalist and also helped promote its own corporate personality.

- When a major business magazine carried a feature on computer risks, management consultancy Arthur Young made available to the writer the results of a detailed survey it had recently conducted in the field. The survey helped to shape the writer's perception of the subject and also provided helpful coverage of Arthur Young's skills in this area.

- A business magazine was carrying a feature on organizing management information – an elusive concept, difficult to get to grips with. A software manufacturer provided an example of how its database management system was being used to deliver real business benefits at Hertz, the car rental specialist. The example became the main focus of the feature and provided valuable publicity for the software company.

- A journalist penning an opinion piece on why companies need an information technology director on their board, sought the views of a consultant at PA Computers and Telecommunications. The consultant provided useful information that strengthened the writer's argument and also revealed PA's own information technology skills.

Remember ... if you know about the purpose of the interview in advance, you will be able to anticipate more easily the line of questioning and thus prepare to present your messages in a way that both reinforces the corporate personality you are seeking to promote and is helpful to the journalist.

3. **What you should know about your company and its messages**

To start with, you should be certain you have all the background information about your company – the kind of information that is too often overlooked – at your fingertips. Check Data Module 16 in Chapter 4 for this information.

Then you need to make sure you know the major proactive messages that your company is seeking to get across. Check Data Module 11 in Chapter 4 for these.

Next, you need to bear both of these in mind as you focus on the purpose of the interview in hand. You need to be certain you are completely up to date on your company's activities in whatever areas will be discussed. And you should try to anticipate the main areas that the interviewer is likely to want to know about and possible questions that may be asked. Remember that an interviewer will often want to probe behind the information you provide. When you volunteer information in an interview, have you thought about the likely supplementary questions it may provoke?

Don't try and prepare answers to all the questions that could be asked. That would probably be impossible, and in any event would lead to a stilted and possibly unproductive interview for both parties. Some journalists requesting interviews with executives may be asked to submit a list of questions in advance. Generally, journalists are reluctant to do this. And, in any event, it gives an impression to the journalist that you're nervous about him or her finding out things about your company that you might wish to hide. But you should arrange to be well briefed on all the main areas that are likely to be discussed.

And it is probably helpful to prepare a form of words to use in answer to questions about any especially sensitive areas. But you should avoid giving the appearance of parroting some kind of company line. You will also create a better impression by not reading from a prepared statement on a particular subject.

Finally, you need to make certain you have assembled everything you are likely to need during the interview before it starts. It gives an unprepared and unprofessional appearance not to have material to hand that an interviewer might reasonably expect you to have. It also wastes time and interrupts the flow of the interview if you have to search around for papers in the middle of it.

The checklist below suggests material that you may want to have to hand. But make sure you provide only the information the journalist really needs rather than a ton of irrelevant bumf.

CHECKLIST 5.2:
MATERIAL TO HAVE TO HAND AT AN INTERVIEW

- Company backgrounder

- Product backgrounders

- Annual report and accounts

- Product/company literature

- Case studies

- Statistics about the company

- Photographs

- Diagrams/charts

- Manager/interviewee biographies

- Relevant quotes

- Names of product users/dealers/etc for further contact

THE NINE MAIN SITUATIONS IN WHICH YOU WILL FACE THE MEDIA

As a company spokesperson, you could meet the media in many different kinds of situations. Some are foreseeable, others unforsee-able. Some are welcome, others less so. There are, of course, many features which apply in all situations which we have already looked at. But there are also special features which apply in different situations and being aware of the opportunities and problems in each different kind of situation will make you more effective as a spokesperson.

The main situations in which you'll meet the media are described in the following checklists.

CHECKLIST 5.3: FACE-TO-FACE INTERVIEW

When it happens

When you set up an interview with a journalist or respond to a request for an interview.

Opportunities

■ Personal contact gives you the chance to put across your message most persuasively. There's nothing like talking to people for effective communication.

■ Meeting a journalist gives you the chance to develop a professional relationship as a springboard for future positive coverage.

Problems

■ The interview could well be lengthy, probing and require detailed responses to questions.

■ Personal like or dislike of the interviewer could colour your response and make your answers too effusive or too reticent.*

---

* Sometimes senior executives – the company chairman, for instance – insist on seeing the editor of a newspaper or magazine. Don't. Editors don't write most of the copy – that's done by other journalists. And don't be surprised if the journalist proves not to be a collar-and-tie man or blouse-and-skirt woman. Some journalists are 'casual' dressers.

CHECKLIST 5.4: TELEPHONE INTERVIEW

When it happens

Generally at short notice from a journalist who wants a speedy response to a question or issue.

Opportunities

■ Gives you the chance to be seen in a positive and responsive light.

■ Frequently provides an opportunity to plug into a story idea a journalist has developed and mould the idea with a message that serves your business objectives.

Problems

■ A real risk of being caught wrong-footed on an issue to which you haven't given proper consideration.*

■ The context of the journalist's story may not be helpful to the message you want to provide.

■ Hasty off-the-cuff comments can give an impression you didn't intend to reveal or facts you would have preferred to remain confidential.

* In rare cases, it has been known for a journalist chasing a difficult story to ring up pretending to be someone they are not. The Press Council was very clear on the subject of subterfuge. Its Code of Practice said: 'Newspapers and journalists serving them should use straightforward means to obtain information or pictures. Their use of subterfuge can be justified only to obtain material which ought to be published in the public interest and could not be obtained by other means.' If in doubt about a caller, ring them back to see if they really are who they claim to be.

CHECKLIST 5.5: PRESS CONFERENCE

When it happens

Usually to make a major announcement or to react to widespread calls from the media for a statement or comment about a particular situation.

Opportunities

- Gives you the chance to prepare and present a message to a wide group of journalists at the same time.*

- Enables you to present a product at first hand or use audio-visual aids to put across your message.

- The status of the event can improve coverage when properly used for major announcements.

Problems

- Unexpected questions can display a weakness in your case to a lot of journalists at the same time – unless there has been careful preparation.

* But not, of course, if the press conference is held in an inaccessible place and at an inconvenient time – especially the day before a publication goes to press. Probably the all-time record for the least attractive press call goes to the Ministry of Defence. *Venue:* The island of Gruinard in the Hebrides. *Purpose:* To declare that ministry 'experts' had declared the island was at last free from the anthrax that poisoned it in 1942. Journalists had to make their own travelling arrangements and, if they doubted the ministry 'experts', provide their own protective clothing.

CHECKLIST 5.6: PRESS BRIEFING

When it happens

At your instigation, normally to make an announcement that is likely to be of interest to a small group of journalists, or to provide background or insight to a development you want publicized, or to take the sting out of some item of negative news affecting your company by providing a broader and more positive context.

Opportunities

■ Gives you the chance to meet a small group of journalists which you select on your terms, sometimes on ground rules you will have defined.

■ Provides the chance to give each journalist a personal face-to-face briefing in sufficient detail to promote the understanding you want to engender.

■ Helps to establish personal relationships with journalists that can be of value in the future.

Problems

■ Journalists interested in a briefing would be likely to be well informed about your industry and/or company and could ask searching and possibly awkward questions.

CHECKLIST 5.7: FACILITY TRIP OR VISIT

When it happens

To show off your factory, office or other facility, or to visit sites of satisfied customers.

Opportunities

■ Provides the chance to show selected journalists the positive side of your company and its activities over an extended period of time, rarely less than a whole day.

■ Shows journalists at first hand what you want them to understand – always more effective than telling them in a remote office.*

■ Gives you the chance to build positive working relationships with journalists you may not have previously known, or only know slightly.

Problems

■ Inadequate preparation can highlight weaknesses rather than strengths.

■ Even with preparation, customers – if it is a customer visit – may not always say just what you'd like them to.

■ Poor travelling arrangements and time wasting irritates journalists.

---

* Although organized in the early 1970s, a press trip run by Philips Computers is still remembered by the journalists who went on it as one of the most effective. Shortly before the introduction of Value Added Tax few people in Britain understood what it was or how it worked – even though most mainland continental countries had operated it for years. Philips took journalists to companies in three countries to show how they operated VAT – all, of course, using Philips computers.

CHECKLIST 5.8: EXHIBITION

When it happens

Whenever you take a stand at an exhibition or organize your own.

Opportunities

■ A chance to meet journalists interested in your industry area that it might otherwise be difficult to get hold of.

■ A chance to show your products and services to journalists on your own terms.

Problems

■ Inadequate arrangements to meet or receive journalists on stands could lead to missed opportunities – or even create bad feeling.*

■ Not all sales people on stands are ideal for discussing company and products with journalists. You should consider whether those likely to meet journalists should be trained as spokespeople.

■ Inexperienced staff could make comments or provide information to journalists that is not helpful to the company.

---

* Journalists particularly dislike vague appeals from public relations consultants days before a major show to join them for a 'glass of champagne' on so-and-so's stand. In too many cases, the purpose of the proposed visit is not clearly stated. Journalists would rather have a story than a glass of champagne – or, preferably, both.

CHECKLIST 5.9: ANNUAL GENERAL MEETING

When it happens

Once a year in every company. Only publicly quoted companies will normally attract press, especially if there is some chance of controversy or 'bad' news.

Opportunities

- Provides an authoritative platform for making statements about a company's future direction.

- The company's top decision-makers have the chance to explain policy and plans in an authoritative gathering in which journalists, unless shareholders, have no legal right to ask questions.

- Provides a chance for the company to address, through the media, the mass of shareholders not at the meeting.

Problems

- Gives disgruntled directors and/or shareholders the chance to meet and put their grievances to journalists.

- The company's top people could be 'ambushed' by journalists for off-the-cuff comments before or after the meeting.

CHECKLIST 5.10: CONFERENCE OR SEMINAR

When it happens

When you or other managers are invited to address a professional or trade gathering or other event.

Opportunities

- Apart from speaking to those present, a speech delivered to an important industry, professional or other event can be of interest to the press.

- Regular speakers at conferences and seminars take on a special aura as 'pundits' or 'gurus' in the eyes of the press and become more 'newsworthy'.

Problems

- Unguarded comments at conferences – especially in answer to questions – can be reported if journalists are present.

CHECKLIST 5.11: DOOR STEPPING

When it happens

Extremely rarely, and often in response to an event of major and newsworthy significance, often a crisis. (Door stepping refers to journalists waiting outside someone's home or office or waiting for them to come off a plane or train in order to ask them questions.)

Opportunities

- By remaining cool, calm and collected, the chance to show you are in control of the situation.

- By being pleasant in trying circumstances, the chance to win personal sympathy for your plight from the public.

Problems

- Appearing flustered by the unwanted attentions of journalists, especially in TV coverage, can give the appearance that you are not in command.

- Throw-away lines in response to shouted questions rarely put your case effectively and can give a grossly misleading impression.

- Displaying hostility to door-stepping journalists may present you in an extremely unfavourable light, especially on TV, and may lose you any residual sympathy from the journalists themselves.

TO SUM UP

In this chapter you've:

- discovered when you need to have information about your interviewer and what you need to know;

- found out about the main purposes that could lie behind a journalist's request to interview you;

- reviewed what you should know about your company and its messages before undertaking an interview;

- studied the opportunities and problems in nine different interview situations.

◀ 6 ▶

Meeting The Media

'There aren't any embarrassing questions – only embarrassing answers.'

Carl Rowan, *The New Yorker*

In 'Meeting the Media' you'll learn about:

> ○ eight rules that will help you make a good impression with journalists;
>
> ○ the essential elements of good interview technique;
>
> ○ how to handle journalists in special situations;
>
> ○ nine guidelines to keep you smiling when you're in the frame.

EIGHT RULES THAT WILL HELP YOU MAKE A GOOD IMPRESSION WITH JOURNALISTS

As we have seen, you will be meeting journalists under a number of different circumstances. There will be special points to bear in mind for some of them. But there are also a number of general rules for creating a good impression with journalists.

Some of these rules may just seem like common sense. But they are mentioned here because they have all been broken at some time – in certain instances, many times – by managers meeting journalists.

CHECKLIST 6.1: GOOD INTERVIEW MANNERS

- **If you have arranged a meeting with a journalist, keep it.** Turn up yourself. Don't send along a deputy.

- **If you have arranged a meeting with a journalist don't keep him or her waiting.** You may think you give an impression of an executive grappling with management problems while the journalist waits in reception. But you don't. You just create an image of bad-mannered boorishness. And you almost certainly get the interview off to a poor start. If punctuality is the politeness of princes, it should also be the politeness of managers.

- **A friendly greeting works wonders.** It creates immediate empathy. It marks you out as one of nature's warmhearted carers. It shows you're looking forward to the meeting and expect it to be useful. So cross the room to greet your interviewer. Get up from behind your desk with a smile on your face and your hand outstretched for a firm shake.

- **Adopt a positive, helpful attitude.** The jounalist wants to meet you and find out about your company. Act as though you want to meet him or her, not as if the interview is an unwelcome intrusion in a busy day. (Even if it is.)

- **Give all your time to your interviewer.** Put calls on hold. Tell your secretary to keep personal visitors in the outer office. Don't sit scanning letters or telexes while answering questions. Don't seem bored. Or rushed. Or look as though there are more important things you could be doing.

- **Make sure you meet in a setting that will do you credit.** If your office is small and untidy reserve a meeting room. Remember, the journalist can write about what he sees as well as about what you tell him. (If you don't want it mentioned, take the pictures of your five previous wives off your desk!)

- **Behave in a way that portrays the style you want to convey.** In the way you treat other members of staff the journalist meets while he or she is with you. In your approach to drivers, doormen and waiters. (Journalists are like receptionists in that they can usually tell who the 'nice' people are.)

- **Moderation pays dividends.** Don't use language that would make a sailor blush – especially with female journalists (although there are one or two who could themselves redden the cheeks of most of the Royal Navy). If entertainment is involved, drink moderately. Even if the journalist doesn't.

THE ESSENTIAL ELEMENTS OF GOOD INTERVIEW TECHNIQUE

Being a good interviewee is not a God-given gift. It is something that can be learned and developed. Nor is there anything mysterious about it. In a world in which business has to put its point of view, ability as an interviewee is another important management skill.

It is important to stress that there are very few 'natural' interviewees. And there is, after all, no reason why being a skilled interviewee should come any more naturally than being a skilled accountant or any other specialist task. With knowledge, technique and training you can become an effective interviewee.

In being a good interviewee, you need to give attention to three main areas. These are:

- what to do during the interview in order to be more effective;

- what not to do during the interview;

- how to handle journalists' ploys which might trap you.

We will now deal with each of these areas in turn.

1. What to do during an interview in order to be more effective

During an interview, you should seek to follow the guidelines set out below in Checklist 6.2.

CHECKLIST 6.2:
WHAT TO DO DURING AN INTERVIEW

- **Tell the truth.** Never be caught in a lie – and, if you try one, you surely will be. The journalist will never completely believe you again. Remember what Mark Twain said: 'When in doubt, tell the truth'.

- **Keep to the point.** If you have done the preparation suggested in the earlier chapters you will know what your point is. Keep to it. Don't wander off or be distracted. If you establish a clear focus, an interviewer will often respond with further questions in that area.

- **Be sure of your facts.** Only provide information that you're certain about. Having to back-track to correct yourself only undermines your authority as an interviewee.

- **Be positive and direct.** Use positive angles for your story. Even if there is a negative aspect to the story, accentuate the positive elements. But avoid unrealistic hype. Or claims you cannot substantiate.

- **Keep your message simple.** Simple messages make the most impact. Few people have the time or inclination to digest the minutiae of a finely developed case.*

- **Be informed and spontaneous.** You will be well briefed, but don't sound as though you are parrotting a company line. Sound as though you actually believe what you're saying. And clearly understand the parameters of the information you want to give – and the information you don't.

- **Light up your message.** Use examples, anecdotes or stories to bring your message to life. Try to find some well-turned phrases to bring your message home powerfully. (But don't go over the top into Churchillian rodomontade.)

- **Let your voice sell your message.** Don't speak in a monotone. Adopt the right tone of voice for the message you're giving in the way you do in ordinary life. But don't try to be Laurence Olivier. That will sound false.

- **Be brief and clear.** When you've made your point, stop. Don't ramble. And don't be ambiguous in your answers. Eschew jargon. Make it clear what you mean.

* A word of advice about simple messages. After listening to his first speech in the House of Commons, David Lloyd George gave this advice to Harold Macmillan: 'Never say more than one thing . . . Of course, you wrap it up in different ways. You say it over and over again with different emphases and illustrations. You say it forcefully, regretfully, even threateningly, but it is a single clear point. That begins to make your reputation.'

- **Use the questions as pegs for your answers.** You know what you want to say. Use the questions to steer towards what you want to say. That means you must listen carefully to the questions and catch any nuances behind them. But don't tell the interviewer what questions to ask. And don't start cross-questioning the interviewer.

- **Look at your interviewer.** Talk to him or her. Listen carefully to nuances behind your interviewer's questions. Eye contact increases rapport between you. And it makes you appear open and honest. (Which, of course, you are!)

- **Tackle distortions or untruths at once.** Don't allow the interviewer to summarize your answers in a way that is not completely accurate or gives your answer an emphasis you didn't intend. Make clear what you mean and what the truth is.

- **Finally, be aware of the dangers of speaking 'off the record'.** Unless you know the journalist well and trust him or her. Even then, be cautious.** Off the record means that what you say is to guide the reporter but should not be written down. But off the record information is known to find its way into stories. Above all, never tell a journalist something – and then add as an afterthought that it was 'off the record'. As a general rule of thumb:

  1. If you don't know the journalist or only know him or her slightly, it is probably wisest only to give off the record information when the alternative is worse. For instance, when off the record information can defuse a potentially damaging story by providing the journalist with an understanding of background facts that will change his or her perception of it.

** US TV reporter Dan Rather gives this advice to politicians (and the same applies to business people). 'In dealing with the press, do yourself a favour. Stick with one of three responses: (a) I know and can tell you; (b) I know and I can't tell you; (c) I don't know.'

2. If you know the journalist well and have developed mutual trust, you can use off the record comments to steer him or her towards a story that may aid your company's business objectives, but with which you would not want to be directly connected.

3. It is worth remembering that some journalists prefer not to have off the record information. They might find out the information elsewhere, and they want to be completely free to use it.*

Remember ... providing 'off the record' information in any situation entails risks. You have to make a judgement as to whether those risks are worth taking given the situation you are in.

2. What not to do during an interview

Interviews can, and do, go wrong. In particular, are a number of common mistakes that managers make when interviewed by journalists. They are summarized in Checklist 6.3 opposite.

* One example of the collective withdrawal from off the record information is *The Independent*'s refusal to attend Downing Street press briefings – the sly nod and wink sessions that press secretaries hold with political correspondents. It is, perhaps, no coincidence that *The Independent* has built up a reputation for breaking big stories from inside Whitehall.

CHECKLIST 6.3: INTERVIEW 'DON'TS'

- **Don't give a journalist information 'not for attribution'.** Except when you are confident the journalist will use it in a way that cannot be traced back to you. The information might not be attributed to you by name. But it could be attributed to a 'company spokesperson' or simply to the 'company', or a 'well-placed source'.

- **Don't 'shoot from the hip'.** You don't have to say the first thing that comes into your mind. If you're asked a tricky question, consider your answer before giving it. If it's a particularly sensitive area, make it clear to the journalist that you want to consider your answer before giving it. As is written in Proverbs 29:11: 'A fool uttereth all his mind; but a wise man keepeth it in till afterward.'

- **Don't get drawn into areas you don't want to talk about.** If the journalist raises subjects you're not happy about discussing – for instance, about the business prospects of competitors – don't be drawn. The journalist may be persistent. (He may try to second-guess you – What will your profit be next year? Will it be more than £10m? More than £20m?) But you must be politely firm.

- **Don't be arrogant or pompous.** You may be an important captain of industry used to commanding legions of minions. But don't show it. In an interview, a touch of humility serves you well. (As Mark Twain said: 'Good breeding consists in concealing how much we think of ourselves and how little we think of the other person.') Don't interrupt when you're being asked questions. And on no account tell the journalist what questions to ask you.

- **Never say: 'No comment'.** In most cases, it is tantamount to admitting guilt. Choose a form of words that explains why you can't comment. For example: 'We haven't decided that yet.' Or: 'We're not making a comment on that until next week.'

3. How to handle journalists' ploys that might trap you

News has been defined as something that somebody doesn't want to tell you. And sometimes it may seem to you that a journalist is more interested in what you *don't* want to tell him or her than what you *do*. Remember what the American film maker Garson Kanin said: 'No one ever won an interview.' Journalists can use a number of ploys to tempt you to tell them more than you meant.

CHECKLIST 6.4: JOURNALISTS' PLOYS

- **The big yawn.** Beware of the journalist who doesn't seem interested in what you're saying. He knows it'll tempt you to make what you're saying more interesting. And in doing that you might reveal facts you meant to keep confidential.

- **The closed notebook.** Just because the journalist shuts his notebook doesn't mean the interview is over. He's still listening to what you are saying. And he can use it in his article.*

- **The 'manufactured' quote.** That's when the journalist tries to put words into your mouth. The journalist starts a question with words like: 'Wouldn't you agree that . . .' and follows it up with some tendentious comments. Never answer a leading question of the 'manufactured' quote variety with a simple 'yes' or 'no'. 'Yes' could be taken as agreement with the proposition. 'No' could be interpreted in a way that you don't regard the subject as important. You should say something like: 'I wouldn't use those

---

* The new chief executive of a big California-based company gave an interview to a British journalist. During the interview, he described how all was sweetness and light when he joined the company. Later, over lunch, he confided that he had had to sack most of the senior management team and close down one plant. The journalist, who didn't open his notebook once during the lunch, still had his story!

words . . .'. And then add: 'The way I would put it . . .', saying what you mean in words you feel comfortable with. How do you spot these loaded questions? They often contain words like 'blame', 'condemn', 'accuse', etc.

■ **The upside-down reader.** If you're consulting documents during your interview – or have other documents on your desk – make sure they are not confidential. Many journalists, particularly those trained in the ancient art of 'subbing on the stone' are experts at reading upside down.

■ **The shoulder to cry on.** A journalist may seem sympathetic to your company and your personal concerns. However, do not treat a journalist – especially over informal drinks afterwards – as a confidant(e) or sympathetic ear for worries or concerns you have about your job, your colleagues or your company.

■ **The red rag.** Don't charge at it when it's waved at you. That's what the journalist wants you to do. If a journalist asks what seems to be rude or hostile questions, he may be trying to provoke you into losing your temper. You might say something then you'd later regret to see in print.**

■ **The smooth talker.** Virtually the opposite of the 'red rag'. The journalist suggests that you're a 'man of the world' or a 'discerning woman'. That you're too clever to believe 'all that'. And then asks: 'So what's the real story?' Stick to your guns.

■ **The bush beater.** A journalist may seem to be spending a lot of time repeating questions in slightly different ways – beating about the bush – or asking similar questions. He or she keeps coming at the same subject from different directions. By worrying away at a topic like this, the

** After losing his temper with famous American newspaper columnist Art Buchwald, James Hagerty, President Eisenhower's press secretary, ruefully reflected: 'If you lose your temper at a newspaper columnist, he'll get rich, or famous, or both.'

journalist is hoping to lull you into a false sense of security. Or he or she may be trying to extract contradictory answers that could be used as the basis for further probing questions. Stick to your guns. Repeat yourself if necessary – and try to move the discussion on by revealing in your answers other interesting areas you would like to discuss.*

■ **The 'when did you stop beating your wife?' question.** There could be some occasions when a journalist will make an accusation – perhaps repeated from another source – which you know to be totally false. But by denying it you could give credence to the allegation. More importantly, you could give the journalist a reason for writing a story of the 'Managers today denied . . .' variety. What to do? Insist on going 'off the record' straight away. Provide the facts to show there is no story. Even if the journalist threatens to run a story saying you declined to comment, keep your counsel. Anything you say on the record will help to prop up the story. And, in many instances, the lack of a suitable quote from you may kill the story anyway.

HOW TO HANDLE JOURNALISTS

In Chapter 5 we identified a number of different situations in which you could meet the media. We will now look at the special circumstances that apply in each of them. We have already dealt with what you need to know in order to deal with face-to-face interviews in this chapter. Guidelines for each of the other main areas are contained in Checklists 6.5 to 6.12, on the following pages.

* The former City editor of a major newspaper has described a pastime his reporters employed on a rare 'slow news' day. They would each telephone a different executive of the same company and ask the same question. The different answers would then be compared for revealing or embarrassing inconsistencies.

CHECKLIST 6.5: TELEPHONE INTERVIEWS

Journalists do much of their information gathering on the telephone. And it is an instrument they are very skilled at using. If you are acting as a company spokesperson, it is highly probable that you will speak to journalists more frequently on the telephone than in any other situation. So bear in mind the following points:

- **When a journalist phones with a query, ask yourself whether you are the right person to comment.** Or should someone else deal with the query? But don't use that as an excuse for not talking to a journalist when it *is* your responsibility. And don't refuse to talk to a journalist just because he or she is on the telephone.

- **Be available.** For journalists up against deadlines, there is nothing more frustrating than people who are always 'in meetings'. If it's at all possible come out of the meeting to take the call. If you can't, find out when the journalist's deadline expires and call back at the earliest opportunity. Make sure that secretaries and switchboard operators are briefed on how to deal with calls from the media and when to interrupt meetings.

- **Before you launch into the detail of the interview, find out this important information:**
    journalist's name;
    publication;
    why he/she is calling you;
    contact number; and
    whether the interview is on the record or attributable.

- **Be aware of the dangers of telephone interviews.** Because you cannot see your interviewer you may be more talkative than usual. Combat the danger of garrulousness by imagining you are talking in front of a colleague.

- **Keep in mind the lack of face-to-face contact.** On the telephone there is no 'body language' to give special emphasis to parts of your message. Nor can you use facial expressions to give shades of meaning to what you say. So make sure everything is crystal clear. Humour, too, can more easily be misinterpreted on the telephone.

- **Don't be rushed.** Take the time to think. If necessary note the question and offer to call back. Consider your response. Get a colleague's view. Make sure you *do* call back.

- **Don't say things for the sake of it.** A busy journalist with a deadline to meet will resent having his or her time wasted. If you've nothing useful to say on the proposed interview topic, say so. Explain why.*

- **Call back.** If you think of something else after the interview has finished, ring again. The reporter will be pleased to hear from you providing you do have useful extra information to give and it is before his or her deadline expires.

Finally, one category of telephone interview that is becoming more common is the telephone interview with a radio station. For further information about this, see Chapter 7.

CHECKLIST 6.6: PRESS CONFERENCES

A press conference could be called by your company in order to make an announcement. Or it could be called in response to a large number of requests from journalists for information about a particular topic or incident – for example, in a crisis. The guidelines below are more applicable to the situation where your company is making the running.

These guidelines do not set out to describe how to organize a press conference. Your public relations professional should be able

* Robert Millikan made this shrewd observation: 'The things that a man does not say often reveal the understanding and penetration of his mind even more than the things he says.'

to advise on that and handle arrangements. Instead, the intention is to make you a more effective spokesperson at the conference.

- **Be clear about the purpose of the conference.** Know what messages you want to get across. (If necessary, refer back to Chapter 4.) Make sure that all participating managers understand what part they must play in formulating and delivering the messages that will be conveyed at the press conference.

- **Be clear what you have to do.** Know what others are doing and how you fit into the overall plan of the conference.

- **Thoroughly prepare your presentation.** Check with other speakers that you're not covering the same ground. Remember you're talking to journalists, not potential customers. They are looking for news. In preparing your presentation:
  put the main point at the front;
  keep it hard and newsworthy, avoiding meaningless product puffery;
  eschew jargon, sales talk, company-speak;
  pack your talk with interesting facts and examples;
  keep to your time limit – not more than 10–15 minutes; and
  beware of humour – it can fall flat.

- **Make sure you have a clearly readable script or notes.** If you have a script, don't read it. Learn it thoroughly, so you only have to refer to it. If you use notes, set them out clearly and make sure all points, facts and examples are included.

- **Prepare any visual aids.** Make sure they add something to, rather than just repeat, what you're saying. Keep them simple.

- **Anticipate any questions you may be asked.** Prepare model answers. Be aware of any difficult or sensitive areas

173

and plan with other managers who will be at the conference how to handle them.

- **Rehearse your speech.** Preferably in the room in which you'll be giving it. Check its timing. Don't overrun.

- **Check your visual aids.** Then check them again. And a third time just before you begin. Make sure the equipment (including the microphone) you'll be using works and you know how to use it.

- **When making your presentation, speak up.** Don't mumble. Oratory, it has been said, is the art of making deep noises from the chest sound like important messages from the brain.

- **Don't be put off by apparent non-interest among reporters.** They're not there to cheer. They like to play their cards close to their chest. Reporters don't generally break into wild applause at the end of a press conference presentation. But a ripple of polite clapping is not completely unknown.

- **At question time keep calm.** Don't be flummoxed by seemingly hostile questions. They're just probing. If you've prepared well, you'll know your answers.

CHECKLIST 6.7: PRESS BRIEFINGS

Because the press briefing, with its small numbers, is less formal than a press conference – it often takes place over lunch or, increasingly, breakfast – it requires a special style.

- **Know who's coming.** Make sure you have the key information about the journalists who'll be present. (See Data Module 17 in Chapter 5.)

- **Tailor your messages specifically for each of the journalists who will be present.** Try to look at your message from the different angles they'll approach it. And be ready to talk about it in those terms.

- **At the event itself, spend a fair amount of time with each journalist.** Don't monopolize one or allow yourself to be monopolized by one. After a fair time, politely extricate yourself and move on to the next person.

- **Be aware of the danger of going beyond your brief.** Especially in the relaxed post-prandial atmosphere of a lunch.*

- **Don't provide accidental quotes through throwaway lines you thought weren't being noted down.** And remember, you're not there to be amusing or entertaining but to achieve a purpose. (That doesn't mean you can't be amusing and entertaining in the service of your purpose.)

* The new US owner of a UK company astonished journalists over drinks after his first press conference by describing some of his New York business ventures. These included being the surprisingly proud owner of run-down apartments from which rents were collected from the unfortunate tenants by sometimes unpleasant means. The company did not receive a good press.

CHECKLIST 6.8: FACILITY TRIPS OR VISITS

This checklist is not intended to show you how to organize a facility trip or press visit. Again, that is a task for your public relations professional. But if, as a manager, you are involved in one, remember the following:

- **Know who's coming.** Brief yourself using Data Module 17 in Chapter 5. Prepare to tailor any messages or information you have to give to them.

- **Thoroughly brief any third parties.** That includes managers in sites visited, customers, user sites, etc. They need to know what's happening, who's coming and to be helped to develop their own messages so that they dovetail with your own.*

- **Rehearse demonstrations.** Don't assume something will work just because it always has. And have a fall-back position if something goes wrong.

* When a major UK software company organized a press trip to its US subsidiary, press officers failed to brief a key Stateside manager carefully enough about the dangers of talking about confidential client projects. During the visit, this errant manager revealed to delighted journalists that IBM's key 'data repository' project, on which the software company had been working, was starting again from scratch. The story made a front-page lead in most of the British computer newspapers and caused IBM considerable embarrassment. *Computer Weekly* headlined its story: 'IBM struggles to salvage data repository'. Other press comments: 'IBM has fallen on its sword'; 'They've taken two below the water line'; 'The repository is in the drunk tank'; 'It's all over the floor'. The story also diverted attention away from the main purpose of the visit.

- **Be friendly to your journalist guests.** But be aware of the dangers of allowing yourself to give away more information than you meant to.

- **Provide the same standard of travel and accommodation facilities for the journalists as for yourself.****

CHECKLIST 6.9: EXHIBITIONS

If you have a stand at an exhibition, your public relations advisers will probably arrange to provide journalists with information in the press office. As a manager, who may be interviewed by journalists at the exhibition, you need to remember the following:

- **Make sure everyone on your stand knows what to do if approached by a journalist.** It is sometimes best if certain individuals are designated with the task of talking to journalists.

- **Make sure those tasked with talking to journalists are briefed thoroughly on the messages that are to be put across.** If several people are talking to journalists, it is important that they sing from the same song-sheet. Make sure they all know what's news – new products, new orders, etc.

- **Have spare press kits on the stand.** Journalists might not have picked yours out from among hundreds in the press room.

- **Make sure those briefed to talk to journalists can be reached easily.** If necessary, organize a rota so that the stand is always manned by a press spokesperson. Or equip

** Don't be like the company chairman who personally hosted a press trip to the US. He travelled in unashamed luxury up-front with the first-class passengers, while the journalists were shoehorned into economy with the backpackers.

spokespeople with bleepers or pagers so they can be quickly located.

- **When a journalist calls on the stand get his or her name, publication and contact number.** Don't lose the information in the clutter on the stand.

- **Take time with journalists on the stand.** Don't make them feel rushed or treat them as second-class citizens to potential customers.

- **Make sure everyone on the stand is aware of the danger of careless talk.** That means everyone from the most junior to the most senior. Overheard comments can give reporters interesting leads into stories you might prefer they didn't know about.

CHECKLIST 6.10: ANNUAL GENERAL MEETINGS

In the UK journalists will generally be present only at the AGM's of public companies. In the US, television cameras have been invited to the annual general meetings of major companies for a number of years. Some companies have used the occasions to make major announcements, while others have found the presence of TV cameras an encouragement to vocal minorities.

- **If you want to use the occasion to address the broader world, make sure you give your remarks a sharp news edge.** Have something positive to say. Quote facts and figures.

- **Brief yourself on potential areas of difficulty.** Be aware of disgruntled shareholders out to cause trouble. Handle them with care. Don't let the press treat any confrontation as a 'David and Goliath' incident, with you as the unfriendly Goliath.

- **Prepare an abstract of the main points of your message and statement.** At certain times of year, financial journalists and editors are inundated with annual reports and accounts, and they may not have time to search through yours for the main points.

- **Do not hold the AGM too late in the day.** The journalists may not have time to file their stories for the following day's papers. (And, by the day after, you're old news.)

- **At a major event, consider providing one or more interview rooms.** These can be used for one-to-one interviews with journalists.

CHECKLIST 6.11: CONFERENCES OR SEMINARS

Addressing an industry or professional conference or seminar can be interesting and potentially useful. Here are some tips.

- **Find out whether journalists are going to be present.** If so, you may need to tailor your remarks accordingly.

- **Be helpful to the press if you want to generate press coverage.** Provide a copy of your speech. Be available for a follow-up interview to provide further information or background after it has finished.

- **Be careful about ambiguity or vagueness.** When journalists are looking for a popular angle in a technical or semi-technical presentation, they can easily get hold of the wrong end of the stick. So be quite clear about what you're saying.

- **Answer questions with care.** If journalists are in the audience you may be limited in the information you can provide in answers – especially about confidential product plans, processes or customers.

CHECKLIST 6.12: DOOR STEPPING

Door stepping – the practice of reporters hanging around your house or office in order to question you as you come and go – normally only happens when things are going wrong.

- **Come and go with dignity.** Don't try to sneak out of back ways. They'll have them covered. Don't run away down the streets. Don't shield your face with newspapers. Your calm dignity will show you're still in command of the situation.*

- **Before you leave or arrive, decide if you want to say anything.** If not, just say 'good morning', 'nice day', etc, but don't get provoked into making even short comments.

- **If you do decide to speak, work out precisely what you want to say.** Then stick to it. Don't get drawn further in no matter how persistent the questioning.

- **When you speak, stop and talk.** Don't be questioned on the move – especially if film or video cameras are present. But when you've said your piece, move purposefully onwards.

- **Be neatly presented and smartly dressed.** Shabby personal appearance creates a bad impression at any time – but especially when you're trying to win sympathy. It could also give an impression of being under pressure and not coping.

- **Be confident.** Appear in control of the situation.

- **Don't get hostile.** Of course, journalists may intrude on your privacy. But you may just have to put up with this. By being friendly or even stoical you can win public sympathy.

---

* During the year-long miners' strike, Ian MacGregor, then chairman of the National Coal Board, made the mistake of trying to avoid reporters and photographers by leaving a meeting with a bag over his head. It was a silly and unnecessary action which gave the wrong impression that he was not in command of the situation.

NINE GUIDELINES TO KEEP YOU SMILING WHEN YOU'RE IN THE FRAME

Very few managers seem to enjoy having their photographs taken. Yet newspapers and magazines are now using more and more pictures of managers.

What too many managers fail to realize is that the picture accompanying an article is an important part of the message. In some cases, it could be *the* most important part of the message. It will certainly be the first part of the message noticed by the reader of the newspaper or magazine.

Some photographers are extremely skilled in taking pictures which portray what they perceive to be the character of the manager they're photographing. Indeed, the best photographers have many tricks for getting people to reveal their character during photo-sessions. For example, the legendary photographer, Karsh of Ottowa, took one of the most famous pictures of Winston Churchill. He achieved the familiar pugnacious scowl on Churchill's face by snatching his cigar out of his mouth, seconds before clicking the shutter.

It is very important that a manager should devote enough time to any necessary photography – and not treat it as an irritating afterthought.

It is especially important to consider ways in which you can help make any photograph underline your message – for example, by being photographed using your product, or visiting part of your plant or factory.

To get the best results, follow the guidelines in Checklist 6.13 opposite.

CHECKLIST 6.13:
BEING PHOTOGRAPHED AT YOUR BEST

■ **Be co-operative.** Help the photographer to get the best picture of you. Don't object if he draws your curtains, moves your chair or shifts around objects on your desk. He's trying to get the best lighting conditions and remove distracting clutter.

■ **But don't be manipulated.** The photographer may want to take an unusual shot. Perhaps with a backdrop of your product or factory. Be sure that it is something you'll be happy with.*

■ **Don't be shy.** Check your tie and hair. Button your jacket. Look the part.

■ **Avoid an audience.** You don't want wise-cracking colleagues looking on.

■ **Avoid a stock shot.** Newspapers and magazines keep stock head and shoulder shots (the boardroom portrait) on file. But they are increasingly looking for something more creative. Pictures that editors hate include:
     executive behind desk;
     executive talking on telephone;
     executives shaking hands; and
     executives signing contracts.

---

* A picture doesn't always tell the true story. Scotland Yard's legendary Detective Superintendent Jack Slipper travelled to Brazil to arrest Great Train Robber Ronnie Biggs amid massive press publicity. But Biggs avoided arrest and Slipper returned without his prisoner. The *Daily Mail* carried a brilliant photograph of a sleeping Slipper on the return flight with an empty seat beside him – the seat meant for Biggs. In fact, the seat wasn't empty. Throughout the flight the seat had been occupied by Slipper's assistant. The *Mail* lensman had snapped the picture when the junior cop momentarily left his seat for the lavatory.

- **Keep your face animated.** But without pulling odd expressions. Politicians, for example, like to be photographed talking because, apart from the fact that it's what they do well, it makes their face look alive.

- **If standing up don't be rigid.** Or adopt an awkward posture. Hold that middle-age spread in.

- **In groups, stand close together.** It makes for the tight shot editors like. And although it may feel strange, it won't look it in the picture.

- **Relax.**

TO SUM UP

In this chapter you've:

- discovered how your approach to the interview can give a good impression to a journalist, and help make the interview a success;

- found out how to make your contribution to an interview more effective;

- reviewed the danger areas in an interview and ways to handle them;

- discovered the ploys that journalists might use to extract more information than you want to provide – and how to handle them;

- reviewed the special guidelines that apply in eight different interview situations;

- found out why a photograph can be an important part of your message – and how to look good in pictures.

◀ 7 ▶

Appearing On Television And Radio

'A word fitly spoken is like apples of gold in pictures of silver.'

Proverbs 25:11

In 'Appearing on Television and Radio' you'll learn about:

○ the steps you should take to develop a company broadcasting policy;

○ how to set the ground rules for broadcast interviews;

○ how to prepare to put your message across most effectively;

○ how to control your nervousness before the interview starts;

○ points that will help you prepare for an interview with confidence;

○ how to be successful during a broadcast interview.

THE STEPS YOU SHOULD TAKE TO DEVELOP A COMPANY BROADCASTING POLICY

Most managers are likely only to be interviewed by print journalists – from newspapers and magazines. It is still the printed publications that contain the largest quantity of news about business and industry.

But it is becoming more likely that you may be interviewed on television or, more probably, radio. The possibility of a radio or TV interview is something that you should not ignore. Why?

- **First, it is a simple question of quantity.** There is now more broadcasting than ever before. More radio stations – especially local stations. And more television stations. Further, they are broadcasting longer hours. They need programmes to fill up the airwaves and business programming is one option.

- **Second, the growth of broadcast media has spawned a new approach to programming – narrowcasting.** When TV stations only broadcast for a limited time each day, most of that time had to be devoted to capturing mass audiences. Now that there are so many hours of broadcasting available, more time can be devoted to appealing to specialized niche audiences: narrowcasting. And one such specialized audience is the business community.

- **Third, even if you are not invited to appear on broadcast TV and radio, you could still find yourself drafted in to appear in a company video.** Or, increasingly, in a videoconference in which some broadcasting skills will help you put across your case to a remote audience.

But before you comb your hair, apply some make-up and step before a camera, it is vital that your company develops a broadcast media policy that determines, among other things:

- when you will allow your managers to appear on radio and television;

- when and where you will allow cameras on your company's premises;

- who is allowed to appear on radio and TV – and under what circumstances.

In order to develop such a policy it is first necessary to be aware of the different circumstances in which you and your company could conceivably be invited on to TV or radio.

CHECKLIST 7.1: OCCASIONS WHEN YOUR COMPANY COULD BE ON TELEVISION

News programmes (national or regional)

- Studio interview (almost always recorded).

- Location interview (on your premises or elsewhere).

- Down-the-line interview (you are interviewed from a remote studio by an interviewer in another studio).

- Telephone interview (rare, but occasionally done). You speak to an interviewer over the telephone while a picture of you or your company's office, etc is on screen.

- Quoted comments (you speak to a reporter who quotes your comments in a scripted news broadcast).

Documentary/actuality programmes

- Studio interview (generally recorded, but on some occasions live).

- Location interview (generally filmed on your premises or elsewhere).

- Studio discussion (recorded or live, generally with a panel, and sometimes with an audience).

CHECKLIST 7.2: OCCASIONS WHEN YOUR COMPANY COULD BE ON RADIO

News programmes

- Studio interview (normally recorded but very occasionally live).

- Location interview (invariably recorded at your premises or another location).

- Telephone interview (at an arranged time you speak to a studio interviewer over a telephone line).

- Quoted comments (you speak to a reporter who quotes your comments in a scripted news item).

Documentary/feature programmes

- Studio interview (either recorded or live).

- Location interview (normally recorded).

- Studio discussion (often with other panel members and either recorded or live).

- Quoted comments (you speak to a reporter or researcher who quotes your comments in the programme).

Phone-in

- Studio-based (you answer questions live from an interviewer and members of the public over the telephone.

With the information contained in Checklists 7.1 and 7.2 in mind, you are now in a position to develop a broadcasting policy for your company. The detail contained in such a policy will vary quite considerably from one company to another. The detail of your company's policy will be determined by factors such as:

- the size of your company;

- the likelihood of its managers being invited to take part in broadcast opportunities; and

- the company's sensitivity to matters broadcast about its activities.

Three points need to be made quite clear.

1. It is possible to find or generate proactive opportunities for positive coverage of your company and its activities. For example, BBC TV's *Tomorrow's World* frequently carries positive stories about companies that are succeeding with new innovative products or techniques. Regional television and local radio programmes are also keen on 'success stories' that foster regional or local pride.

2. There may, however, be times when the broadcast media is interested in a story that is not helpful to your corporate personality or business objectives. In these cases, there is no point in imagining that if you ignore the broadcast media they will go away and not bother you. You need to meet the challenge and seek to limit the damage.

3. Often, radio and TV broadcast news organizations will be interested in your company when things are going wrong – rather than right. Too often, they regard 'bad' news as the best news.

Bearing these points in mind, you can develop the framework of a broadcasting policy for your company, by answering the questions posed in Data Modules 18 and 19 on the following pages.

Remember ... when you have drawn up your company broadcasting policy make sure that all managers know about it. It should be written down and circulated to those managers who may take decisions, so that there is no doubt or confusion over what the policy is.

DATA MODULE 18: WHICH MANAGERS ARE ALLOWED TO COMMENT ABOUT WHICH SUBJECTS ON RADIO AND TELEVISION

Subject	Named spokespeople	TV	Radio
Corporate affairs (ie financial results, acquisitions, etc)	——————— ———————	[ ] [ ]	[ ] [ ]
Policy issues (ie impact of government policy, etc)	——————— ———————	[ ] [ ]	[ ] [ ]
Products	——————— ———————	[ ] [ ]	[ ] [ ]
Community issues (ie relationship with local communities)	——————— ———————	[ ] [ ]	[ ] [ ]
Labour relations	——————— ———————	[ ] [ ]	[ ] [ ]
Environmental/ Green issues (ie pollution)	——————— ———————	[ ] [ ]	[ ] [ ]
Legal issues	——————— ———————	[ ] [ ]	[ ] [ ]
Crisis spokesperson	——————— ———————	[ ] [ ]	[ ] [ ]
Other (specify)	——————— ———————	[ ] [ ]	[ ] [ ]

DATA MODULE 19: WHEN AND WHERE CAMERAS WILL BE ALLOWED ON COMPANY PREMISES

Are cameras allowed on all our premises?   Yes/No

If not, where are they *not* allowed?   _____
                                         _____
                                         _____
                                         _____

Are there any restrictions when cameras may be on our premises?   Yes/No

If so, what are they?   _____
                         _____

Who is authorized to give permission for filming?   _____
                                                      _____
                                                      _____

Will we supply our products for filming?   Yes/No

Can our products be filmed on user sites?   Yes/No

If so, where?   _____
                 _____

HOW TO SET THE GROUND RULES FOR BROADCAST INTERVIEWS

As with most types of interview, there are three kinds of situations in which you may find yourself on TV and radio.

- **Proactive:** where you are putting across a positive message.

- **Reactive:** where you are responding to requests for information or comment. In broadcasting this can often mean defending yourself or your company against criticism – but not always.

- **Crisis:** where you are providing information in response to a dramatic event – sometimes a disaster. (This will be dealt with specifically in Chapter 8.)

It is, of course, important to prepare for all types of interview. Indeed, it is especially important that you prepare for what you imagine will be the positive kind of interview. Far too many company spokespeople have shot themselves in the foot because they thought what seemed like a positive opportunity was going to be an easy ride.

However, it is also the case that there are an increasing number of occasions on both TV and radio when a company spokesperson has to defend his or her company against criticism or allegations. Both TV and radio lend themselves to a more dramatic adversarial approach to news and features than print journalism. And there is a growing interest both from news programmes and documentaries about 'investigative' stories concerning business. For example, Roger Cook, of *The Cook Report*, showed, first on radio and then on television, that chasing after crooked business people makes good entertainment – as well as good journalism. Other television programmes with a consumerist slant are *Watchdog*, *4 What It's Worth* and *That's Life*.

The first thing to remember if your company is targeted by an investigative programme with a potentially negative impact is that your company is not powerless. So, instead of sitting transfixed like a snake mesmerized by a mongoose, you should act to ensure that your company is presented in the best possible light.

You need to set the ground rules for any interviews or feature filming that might be required at your company.

The first step is to find out what the programme is about and what specific interest the programme makers have in your company. You should also ask them why they want an interview or filming facilities. And it does no harm at all to ask them to put that information in writing. Then you both know where you stand.

The second step is to decide whether or not you want to take part in the proposed programme. As a general rule, if specific allegations are to be levelled against your company, there are very few cases when you should decline an invitation to take part outright. In those cases, the programme makers will almost always state in their programme that you refused to take part and the refusal may be presented in such a way as to make you look guilty.

In fact, it is your duty to your company – however difficult or troublesome – to co-operate with the programme makers and make sure that your company's case is put in as positive a manner as possible.

In doing this it is helpful to adopt the following four-point approach.

1. Be certain you are fully aware of as many facts about the programme/news item as possible

- What precisely will it be dealing with?

- Why was the subject chosen? What events or circumstances have brought it about?

- What is the editorial point of view of the programme/ presenter?

- In what context will the items in question appear?

- Who else (especially critics) will be given air time in the programme?

- What specific allegations/criticisms are likely to be made about your company?

- When will the programme be broadcast?

- Who is likely to see/hear it?

- What groups could have a strong interest and perhaps strong feelings on the matter, ie who could you possibly annoy?

2. Prepare a thorough background briefing about the topic from your company's point of view

- What are the precise facts of the case?

- What corporate policies and/or business objectives are at stake?

- How has the situation arisen?

- What is the background history to the situation?

- What research, etc exists to throw light on the situation?

- What is the company on record as having said about the issue?

- What is the experience of other companies in this country and abroad in a similar situation to your own?

- Are there any special circumstances, such as a legal case pending or an investigation in progress, that would make it inappropriate to comment?

3. Share your background research with the programme makers in order to alter their perspective of the topic

- Remember that programme makers have a duty to be fair and only to make criticisms/allegations in the light of known facts. (If they don't know the true facts they might make the allegations out of ignorance rather than malice.)

● Even someone with an entrenched point of view can't argue with facts when those facts show their view to be erroneous.

● Programme makers usually want to get the true facts. They don't want to present a point of view that is later shown to be at fault.

● Co-operating fully, even – perhaps especially – when you are under attack wins goodwill and sympathy when it's your turn to have your say.

● But don't confuse with too much detail. Concentrate on the points you want to correct and marshal all information to that aim.

● If you have agreed to be interviewed, keep something up your sleeve for the interview. Don't let it out in advance – especially any bull points you propose to make to rebut known criticisms.

4. Establish clearly what control you will have over your contribution to the programme

● If it is a feature programme will you have the opportunity to view the programme before it is broadcast in order to see how your contribution is presented in relation to that of others?

● In the case of extremely sensitive issues, it may be essential to make this a pre-condition of taking part in the programme.

● In exceptional circumstances, it may be necessary to get your lawyers to draw up an agreement with the broadcasting authorities to entrench your rights to view the programme before transmission and to insist on a change to any section of your interview that you feel has been unfairly presented either due to editing or unreasonable juxtaposition with other matter.

As you will see, doing all this will take up considerable time and effort – not to mention money. However, not to do it could be to invite disaster. The nature of broadcasting is such that a casual approach almost always ends in catastrophe.

HOW TO PREPARE TO PUT YOUR MESSAGE ACROSS MOST EFFECTIVELY

In preparing to put your message across effectively in a radio or TV interview, there are two main areas you need to consider:

- the actual circumstances of the interview – and how you can turn them to your advantage;

- the points you want to put across in your interview – and the way to put them across most effectively.

1. Check out thoroughly the actual circumstances of the interview

Before you step before the cameras, it is vitally important that you should know precisely what is going to happen and how. You will need to find out the following.

- **Whether the interview will take place in a studio or on location.** In general an interview that takes place in a studio or calm office is better than an interview that takes place in the street, on the doorstep or some other public spot. For a start, you will have far fewer distractions – and, in many cases, so will the viewer (no people pulling funny faces behind the camera!). You should not agree to do the interview in any place that you feel uncomfortable about. And you should be especially wary of allowing the producer/director/interviewer to manoeuvre you into a position which will show you in an embarrassing or poor light. In cases where what is happening outside is the main point of the story – and usually when the story is a positive one – there is a stronger case for conducting the interview outdoors.

- **Whether you will be interviewed alone or with others.** If you are being interviewed with someone else, the chances are that the other person is there to provide an alternative view. You need to know who they are and the points they might make so that you are ready to counter them.

- **How long the proposed interview will be.** Important, since this will influence the way you present your message. As a very general rule of thumb, typical lengths for broadcast interviews are:

    radio news – 1–2 minutes;

    TV news – 30–40 seconds (but can be shorter!);

    feature – up to 3 minutes.

    You will see from these that you must be able to make your points briefly. (This will be discussed in more detail below.)

- **Who the interviewer will be.** Different interviewers have different styles – and pet hobby horses – so it is useful to be aware of these in advance.

- **Whether the interview will be live, taped or filmed.** On both radio and TV, a live interview creates immediate impact, but leaves you with little or no control. There is, obviously, no chance of editing after the event. (But that cuts both ways for the interviewer and the interviewee.) A live interview is more likely on radio than TV. In a live interview it is essential that you get your message across in the time available. When the time is up, the interviewer will cut you off, whether you've finished or not.

    A filmed interview can be edited. So can a videotaped interview. But editing has traditionally been a more cumbersome process with videotape than with film. With either a taped or filmed interview there is always the possibility of doing it again, given the goodwill of the interviewer, which may not always be forthcoming. But editing afterwards means that some of your remarks can be cut. It is, therefore, strongly advisable to limit yourself as closely as possible to the actual time that it is proposed to broadcast.

With film, the programme maker also has the option of filming with or without location sound. In certain situations you could be filmed without location sound. The programme maker will then add commentary over the film in the studio. In that situation, it is useful to know what that commentary will be about. You don't want to create a situation where you have provided the pictorial half of an unhelpful piece.

2. Thoroughly prepare the points you want to put across in your interview

Even in an interview of 2 to 3 minutes, you will not have time to make more than a couple of points – three at the most. In a 40-second interview, you can realistically make only one point. And, it must be added, in an even shorter 'sound bite' you might only have time for one or two sentences.

All this means that you simply cannot afford to step before the cameras unprepared. You must know what you want to say in advance – and how you are going to say it.

- **First, write down in not more than 20 words each of the three most important points you want to make.**

- **Look at them.** Are you sure they are the three most important points? (While you do this consider the audience you'll be reaching. Look at what you have to say from their point of view.)

- **Next, decide on the key facts or examples that support your main points.** Again, be brief. Use only one fact or simple example for each point.

- **Work out how you can use that fact or example to get across your point.** Use simple, direct language. Are your points clear, forceful and unambiguous? Are they in tune with your company's policy?

- **Make a note of likely questions you could be asked.** Work out how in answering those questions you could make the key points you have already defined. What is the question you would least like to be asked? How would you answer it?

- **Finally, what is your most important point?** If you only get the chance to say two sentences, what will they be?

It is important to go through this exercise in order to prepare what you want to say. But there is an important caveat. When you are interviewed you must not sound as though you have learned what you want to say parrot-fashion. You must retain a flexible mind and you must be thoroughly aware of all the background issues surrounding your key points. And you must have thought through how to link your key points *naturally* to any likely questions – hostile or otherwise – that may be asked.

> **Remember ...** when faced with the task of doing a broadcast interview you must, no matter how short the proposed interview, prepare thoroughly what you want to say.

HOW TO CONTROL YOUR NERVOUSNESS BEFORE THE INTERVIEW STARTS

The success or failure of an interview is often determined before it starts. Partly in the briefing and planning. Partly in the care you take in presenting yourself. And partly in the mental attitude with which you approach the interview. A Latin motto may help to stiffen your sinews: 'Necessity makes even the timid brave.'

It is no use pretending that you won't be nervous. Most people are nervous before an important event. Even skilled interviewees who've been through the mill dozens of times, get nervous. It is said that consummate political performer Harold Macmillan used occasionally to be physically sick before prime minister's question time. A cabinet colleague, an 'old pro', who had been in TV interviews many times, took fright during one interview and ran off to hide, shivering behind a curtain.

Not all nervousness is bad. That tingle of anticipation which gets the adrenalin pumping in just the right quantities is likely to give you the edge to perform at your best. (In fact, if you weren't even a little bit nervous, that might itself be a cause for concern.) But overwhelming nervousness, complete with the three Ss – stammers, stutters and the shakes – is destructive. And you must do something to control it. The best place to start is by analyzing the cause of your nervousness.

- **First, it is the worry of the unknown.** But you will have overcome that by collecting all the information about the interview, the circumstances surrounding it and knowing what is expected of you.

- **Second, it is the fear of failure.** You will have tackled that one by briefing yourself thoroughly on the subject of the interview. You will know the three points you want to get across. You will have chosen the outline form of words that will best get them across – complete with examples. You will be thoroughly briefed on the background facts. You will have considered the difficult questions that could be asked – and have your counters ready.

- **Third, it is the anticipation.** It is the time spent sitting in the trenches that builds nervousness, not the actual going over the top. So before setting off for the studio, while travelling to it, and while waiting for the interview to start, you need things to keep you occupied. For example, you will want to look over your briefing materials so that they are completely fresh in your mind.

There are other things you can do to combat the physical symptoms of nervousness.

CHECKLIST 7.3:
WAYS TO COMBAT SYMPTOMS OF NERVOUSNESS

- **Think positive.** Don't get into a negative frame of mind. Your preparation should give you confidence.

- **Breathe deeply.** Your body needs oxygen to function at maximum efficiency. Steady breathing makes you feel better.

- **Take a brisk walk.** It burns up the adrenalin which is helping to make you feel nervous. And it tunes up your body.

- **Loosen your face muscles.** It is important that your face should be animated. So before the interview try some 'silent yawning' exercises. And loosen your neck and shoulder muscles with circular shoulder movements.

- **Stop your hands shaking.** Clench and unclench your fists to control your hand and wrist muscles.

- **Note the position of the lavatory!** If your nervousness makes you want to use it more than normal, knowing where it is removes some of the anxiety.

ELEVEN POINTS THAT WILL HELP YOU PREPARE FOR AN INTERVIEW WITH CONFIDENCE

In preparing for an interview, take account of the following points.

- **Consider your appearance.** Television is largely about images. If you are only on screen for a minute or two, or possibly only a few seconds, most people may only remember the impression you left, rather than your specific message. That impression is partly created by what you look like and partly by how you conducted yourself on screen. Does your hair need washing or trimming? Do you need a shave? Are your clothes clean, tidy and uncrumpled? But don't go over the top: you don't want to look like a B-movie matinee idol or a Hollywood starlet.

- **Dress appropriately.** Men should wear a suitable suit, shirt and tie. The suit should not contain a fine pattern that will strobe on screen. The shirt should not be white – pale blue is a good colour. The tie should not draw attention to itself. If you do the interview standing, button your jacket – it makes you look neater and gives an air of authority. For women, a dress or skirt and blouse and/or jacket comes across best for a business person. Strong colours like red and blue are said to work well on television. In general, avoid heavy jewellery unless you're a fashion designer, artist, actress or jeweller.

- **Arrive in plenty of time.** Allow time for finding a parking place, and for meeting your interviewer beforehand. You don't want to be hanging around for a long time before your interview – that builds up unhelpful tension. But you don't want to rush in at the last moment out of breath and sweating.

- **Meet the people involved in the interview.** This is helpful in getting their measure before they start to interview. It can also be of value in helping them to rectify any errors or misconceptions they may have had about you before you go on air or on screen.

- **Find out how you'll be introduced.** In a panel discussion, studio interview or similar programme, find out the exact words the programme presenter will use to introduce you. Sometimes they will volunteer this information. It is by no means unusual for errors to creep in, and it can be awkward if they're not sorted out before the interview starts.

- **Probe the interviewer's line of questioning.** Try to find out if the interviewer is going to adopt a particular slant. Sometimes that slant may be unhelpful and you may be able to persuade the interviewer to amend it. In any event, you will be forewarned.

- **Ask the interviewer for the exact words of the first question.** He or she might not tell you. But if he or she does you will be able to fashion your first answer to fit the question. Often, the first question will be probing or even hostile. But don't plan to chase after all the negative nuances in it (although correct anything that is blatantly wrong). Instead, plan to put your own positive line.

- **Keep your own counsel.** Don't reveal what you intend to say before the interview starts. If you have some bull points and let the interviewer know about them, he or she may think of questions that undercut what you had to say.

- **Accept make-up.** It can make a significant difference to your on-screen appearance by removing the appearance of moist upper lips, jowly jaw-lines and shiny foreheads, etc.

- **Don't bother about technicalities.** It is not your job to worry about whether the interviewer's tape recorder is working properly or whether the lights are in the right place. Leave that to the experts and concentrate on your own performance.

- **Beware of 'hospitality'.** At some studios you'll be offered alcoholic drinks beforehand. Stick to one (small) one. Or better still none. You may think alcohol will give you Dutch courage. But the signs of drink show up very quickly on television – in your eyes. A drink of sweet tea will increase your blood sugar level and moisten a possibly dry mouth.

HOW TO BE SUCCESSFUL DURING A BROADCAST INTERVIEW

The key features of television news and – to a certain extent documentary programmes – are that they are fast moving, concerned with visual images and controversial. (Controversy makes good television.) Because radio has only sound to convey its message, it is not concerned with images and there is normally more time to make points verbally. Nevertheless, it can still be fast moving and controversial.

You should pay special attention to the following points in order to improve your performance in broadcast interviews. (Not all the points here apply to radio, but those which do are fairly obvious.)

- **Get off to a good start.** The first answer is crucially important, especially in a short interview. But in any interview it will set a standard by which your audience will judge you. That's why it is important to know what the first question will be, if at all possible, and to fashion your answer in advance.

- **Be sincere and truthful.** Television, with its probing eye, exposes insincerity mercilessly. You must believe in what you say. You must be truthful. If you can't do both those things, it is much better not to appear on television at all.

- **Ignore distractions.** In a studio there will be people all around you, doing their jobs, moving equipment, signalling to one another. Ignore them. Don't even try to watch what they're doing out of the corner of your eye. Focus your attention solely on your interviewer.

- **Talk to the interviewer.** He or she is asking you questions. Your answers should be addressed back to the interviewer. Or in a panel discussion, to the chairperson. Don't talk to the camera. Or worse still, a vague spot somewhere in the studio. But, remember, as you talk to the interviewer, you are really talking through him or her to the audience beyond. And your answers should be fashioned with that in mind.

- **Don't let the interviewer bully you.** He or she may be asking you probing or even downright hostile questions. Don't be intimidated. Stand up for yourself. Put your point of view forcefully but fairly. Do not be goaded into losing your temper or hurling cheap abuse. Remember former Secretary of State for Defence, Sir John Nott, who did not enhance his reputation with many viewers when he was shown storming out with the words 'I'm not putting up with this', during a testing interview with Sir Robin Day. You gain points with the viewer or listener by keeping cool and collected under fire. On the other hand, don't adopt a matey tone with the interviewer. Keep your relationship formal and businesslike.

- **Be serious.** In an interview about a serious subject, you should treat all questions seriously. Don't assume any questions have been flippant – even if they sound it. Don't try to be funny: that almost always backfires.

- **Don't make off-the-cuff comments.** You should have prepared what you want to say beforehand. Stick to it. Don't introduce points you've just thought of. Avoid the temptation to make policy on your feet. Especially avoid making instantaneous analogies. They may contain shades of meaning you hadn't considered and give a wrong – perhaps seriously wrong – impression. Analogies are double-edged weapons. Harold Wilson learned that lesson when he told voters that 'the pound in your pocket' had not been affected after its devaluation. That phrase returned to haunt him for years as inflation grew.

- **Firmly correct any inaccuracies.** Do not let any important factual inaccuracies from the interviewer or anyone else taking part in the programme go unchallenged. Otherwise the viewer will assume they are correct. Generally, make the correction in the first words you say as soon as it is your turn to speak. (It is only a good idea to interrupt in exceptional circumstances, but if the interviewer is saying something wrong you could indicate your disagreement by shaking your head. The viewer can then see that you don't agree.)

- **Look relaxed.** Even if you aren't! Give yourself a quick visual check just before the interview starts to make sure hair is in place, tie straight, jacket buttoned, and so on. If you are doing the interview standing, don't fidget from one foot to another. Hold your arms in a relaxed fashion at your side. If sitting, sit up straight with legs together. Don't wriggle in your seat. In an interview close-up you can move your head a reasonable amount, but try to keep your body fairly still. Throughout an interview, use only the absolute minimum of hand gestures.

- **Sound interested.** If you don't sound as though you're interested in what you're saying, nobody else will be. That means keeping your voice bright and fresh. But avoid histrionics.

- **Finish strongly.** Know the length of the interview and judge when it is coming to a close. Watch for wind-up signals from the studio manager (the one instance when you should take quarter of an eye off the interviewer – but not while you're answering a question). Watch for these signals from the studio manager: one finger up – one minute to go; arms crossed in front of chest – half a minute to go; circular motion with hand – come to a close; one-arm waving motion at shoulder level – finish at once. Get a strong bull point into your last answer – if necessary by repeating in new words something you have already said.

CHECKLIST 7.4: SPECIAL POINTS TO CONSIDER DURING A TELEVISION INTERVIEW

In addition to the general points listed above, which apply to both television and radio, it is also advisable to bear in mind the following if you are involved in a television interview.

- **Look at the interviewer.** You are having a conversation with him or her. Don't glance about you. The movement of your eyes is especially noticeable on a television screen. If you keep looking around, you will either look stupid or devious.

- **Sit upright.** Don't slump. But be comfortable. Let your hands rest in your lap.

- **Project your personality.** You don't want to go over the top. But if you are too 'laid back' you'll just seem flat and the viewer will lose interest in what you're saying.

- **Don't take notes.** It's distracting. All the information you need should be in your head.

- **Be alert at all times.** The camera could switch to you at any moment.

- **Control irritating mannerisms.** If you tend to wiggle your ears or have other annoying habits – don't. And try not to touch your face too much. It doesn't look good on screen.

- **Be aware of time.** You should know how long your interview is due to last. Be aware when it is ending so that you can finish on a strong point.

- **Listen carefully for question changes during 'cut-aways'.** During filmed interviews the interviewer will re-film some of his or her questions after the interview is finished. That's because the camera has been on you during the interview. Listen carefully for any changes in the question on this re-filming. Sometimes reporters 'harden' the question which can have an adverse effect on the answer you have just given. Don't be afraid to protest loudly if this happens.

You could be asked to do an interview from a remote studio. In this case, you will find yourself in a room with a camera pointing at you. You'll hear the interviewer's questions over a loudspeaker or through an earplug. Remember the following.

- **Talk to the camera.** Treat it as a person.

- **Make your face react to the question.** (But don't pull

faces!) The camera will often be on you while it is being asked.

■ **Speak in a normal conversational tone.** Treat the interviewer as though he were in the same room with you.

CHECKLIST 7.5: SPECIAL POINTS TO CONSIDER DURING A RADIO INTERVIEW

During a radio interview, bear in mind the following additional points.

■ **Explain clearly what you mean.** Remember that you can't use visual face signals to hint at your meaning as with television.

■ **Keep your answers sharp and to the point.** It's very easy to edit the tape of a radio interview. And this will happen if you ramble.

■ **Don't be afraid of mistakes.** If you make a mistake, ask to do it again. Or if you make a slip in a sentence, just say 'Sorry, that's wrong' and repeat the sentence correctly. The reporter will edit out the wrong sentence later. (Obviously, that is not an option in a live interview.)

■ **Do your interview somewhere quiet.** A lot of background noise can be distracting, unless the noise is actually adding 'location colour' to the piece.

■ **Don't make unnecessary noise yourself.** While being interviewed in a studio, don't rustle paper, bang on the table, knock the table leg or make other background noises. They are amplified on radio and sound awful.

■ **Call back if you are asked to do a telephone interview.** It gives you time to gather your thoughts.

■ **If involved in a phone-in programme, listen care-**

fully to the questions through your headphones. Flatter the questioners, even when they're stupid. Give your answers in a conversational way. Never lose your temper. Learn from the politician doing badly on a local radio phone-in programme who found his fortunes suddenly changed when a rather childish contributor called him 'a cabbage' and then slammed the phone down. The politician treated the incident as a joke – and started to come across as a rather likeable person rather than just another town hall bureaucrat.

TO SUM UP

In this chapter you've:

- discovered why your organization needs to develop a broadcasting policy so it is not caught unawares;

- learned about the four points you need to consider when agreeing to the ground rules for a broadcast interview;

- found out how to control your nervousness before broadcast interviews;

- reviewed the 11 points you should check before an interview starts;

- learned about ways that will help you perform better while the interview is taking place;

- found out about the special points you need to bear in mind when appearing on television or radio.

◀ 8 ▶

Communicating In A Crisis

❝When written in Chinese, the word crisis is composed of two characters – one represents danger and the other represents opportunity.❞

John F Kennedy

In 'Communicating in A Crisis' you'll learn about:

o why crisis communication is different;

o how careful planning helps you deal with crisis;

o the three steps to take to prepare for communicating in crisis;

o eight ways to get fair-minded people on your side in a crisis.

WHY CRISIS COMMUNICATION IS DIFFERENT

Your attitude may be: 'It can't happen to me.' Well, it can. That is why crisis communication skills are important to the company spokesperson.

Of course, nobody *wants* a crisis. And most companies plan to ensure they never get one. But at some stage in its life a company will almost certainly face a crisis of one kind or another. And with crises, lightning can strike twice in the same place. A Midlands-based company involved in metals suffered two accidents. One was an explosion that caused a fatality. The company was besieged by the press but could only provide an unhelpful 'no comment'. A year later there was a fire on the same site. Once again, the company failed to deal effectively with the media and was pilloried in the press.

Some companies are more vulnerable to crises than others. They include companies in the transport industry, companies handling or processing dangerous commodities such as chemicals or oil, companies with intrinsically dangerous manufacturing processes, or those providing mass consumer goods or food products where faulty merchandise could harm customers. That list doesn't exclude many companies.

And even those not included on that list could face crises. Their offices or factory could be burned down. They could be the victim of a major robbery. They could be on the receiving end of a hostile takeover bid. There could be fraud, lawsuits or major computer failures to cope with. And there is a chilling statistic: of 3,336 terrorist incidents logged by the CIA and the US Department of Defence during the 1970s and 1980s, 36 per cent affected business people and property.

This chapter cannot show you how to draw up a complete crisis plan. Instead, it concentrates on the communications aspects of the crisis plan and the spokesperson's role in it.

So, how is crisis communication different from other kinds of corporate communication?

- **First, crisis news is bad news.** It is about something

that is likely to have an adverse effect on your organization.

- **Second, people get hurt.** It is often about something that endangers or damages third parties – physically, spiritually or financially. Not invariably, but in 8 cases out of 10. And sometimes, it tragically involves injury or death to employees, customers or others. For example, one of the worst tragedies ever occurred at Bhopal, India in 1984. Poison gas leaked from an underground storage tank at Union Carbide's plant, killing more than 2,000 and injuring more than 20,000 people. Union Carbide reacted by flying medical supplies, respirators and doctors to the site. And chairman Warren Anderson flew direct to Bhopal, even though he knew he would be arrested by the Indian authorities.

- **Third, you can't keep quiet about it.** No matter how much you might want to hush it up, it's going to be news. Other people know about it. Journalists will write about it. And there's nothing you can do about that.

- **Fourth, you can be on the wrong end of the law.** Increasingly your company or some of its managers could find themselves involved in civil or even criminal proceedings as a result of what has happened. Tougher legislation in many fields and a greater willingness by the courts to pin the blame of liability on companies and its executives now make this more likely.

As a result, your company must have a crisis plan prepared – and part of that plan must be a crisis communication plan. The company spokesperson must be a member of the crisis planning team, and have anticipated what may be required in a given crisis.

Remember ... because you won't have time to prepare when an individual crisis strikes, you must have done your preparation for communicating in possible crises well in advance.

In fact, your preparation for crisis starts with the honest, open and ethical way you run your business. (Socrates had the right idea. He said: 'The way to gain a good reputation is to endeavour to be what you desire to appear.') If your company has by its actions over the years built up a good reputation, it will be in a far stronger position to deal with a crisis when it comes. You will have already built up a bank of goodwill on which you can draw. A particular event could then be seen as an exception to the rule, as bad luck for a well-managed company, rather than as evidence of general poor management or slack procedures.

In fact, a well thought-out and managed communication campaign over the years will also help to build the kind of corporate personality that can withstand severe buffeting from the very occasional crisis event. Just as a court of law looks with greater favour on a transgressor of previous good character, so the public at large is prepared to make allowances for a comany that has a favourable corporate personality.

A crisis doesn't have to be fatal to business if you react sensibly. When botulism from tinned salmon killed two people, John West's business faced disaster. The company re-established the reliability of its product by setting up a canned salmon consumer bureau. It gave out sober facts about its product to consumers, the grocery trade and public health officers. Within two years, sales were back to normal.

HOW CAREFUL PLANNING HELPS YOU DEAL WITH CRISIS

Careful planning can't always avert a crisis, but it may contain it. It can help to avoid a crisis within a crisis – the panic that grips an organization when it doesn't know what to do or when events develop their own self-propelled momentum. What planning can do is to anticipate and possibly channel the shock-waves of a crisis.

The starting point is to identify the danger 'hot spots' in your organization. It's time to think the unthinkable. What really could go wrong? Face up to your worst nightmares. What would you do if they happened?

Ask yourself the following questions.

CHECKLIST 8.1:
QUESTIONS TO ASK WHEN PLANNING FOR CRISIS

- What could happen?

- How could it happen?

- Where might it happen?

- When might it happen?

- Who would be directly affected?

- What about the indirect effects?

- Who else would be concerned?

- What criticism could we face?

- And from which quarters?

- Would laws be broken?

- What would we need to do to put it right?

- And who would need to be involved in doing so?

- How much would it cost?

- Could we afford that kind of money?

- Frankly, could we cope?

By asking and answering the questions in Checklist 8.1 you should have identified the issues that need to be resolved when you draw up a crisis plan.

It is not, of course, the task of the company spokesperson (or people) to take sole responsibility for drawing up a crisis plan. But the spokesperson should have considerable input on those elements of the plan that will involve dealing with the media.

And be in no doubt about how important that is in your crisis planning. To a large extent, when crisis strikes you will be judged not by how you deal with the crisis, but by how you are *seen* to be dealing with the crisis.

In some instances, a badly handled response can trigger a more severe crisis than the initial catalyst. It is all too easy to get dragged into a situation, where you have to devote great efforts to 'explaining away' unfortunate comments already made. Naturally that is a distraction from getting to grips with the underlying problem.

> **Remember . . .** your response to a crisis – what you say and what you do – can be as newsworthy and as potentially damaging as the original crisis itself.

THE THREE STEPS TO TAKE TO PREPARE FOR COMMUNICATING IN CRISIS

As spokesperson, you will need to be certain that all the back-up you need will be in place should you be called on to perform during a crisis. There are three areas to which you should give particular attention in your advance crisis planning.

1. Plan to set up and resource a crisis command centre

Your company should make contingency plans to set up a crisis command centre, either at your corporate headquarters or near the site of the crisis incident. As the spokesperson, you need to be part of that command centre.

The plan for the contingency centre, along with the full crisis plan, needs to be put in writing. Every person responsible for an aspect of the plan needs to know clearly what his or her responsibilities will be in advance. The plan needs to be tested.

As a crisis spokesperson, you need to be certain in advance that your crisis command centre has the following.

- **Adequate telephone lines.** For incoming and outgoing calls.

- **A 'quiet room'.** Away from the bustle of the main activity, where you can draft statements and press releases and consider your next moves.

- **Extra support.** To ensure that calls from journalists can be fielded, if necessary, around the clock. (Journalists don't keep office hours, and journalists from overseas – in different time zones – may also be calling you.)

- **A call-out plan.** To make sure you can get hold of all the people you might need at any hour of the day or night, any day of the year.

- **Procedures and processes.** To ensure necessary and relevant resources and information can be accessed and routed to your crisis command centre as and when needed.

2. Plan to set up a crisis press centre

In a crisis, you will be deluged with requests for information from journalists. You will have to give press conferences – and you will need somewhere to hold them. You will also score brownie points with journalists if you make it easier for them to file stories by providing them with telephones and, possibly, typewriters.

It is possible that your press centre will be at your corporate headquarters. But it is more probable that it will be near the site of the crisis incident. In your crisis communications planning, you should have made contingency arrangements with a nearby hotel, hall or branch office to provide accommodation at short notice for a press centre.

You should try to avoid setting up the crisis centre actually at the site of the incident. That can be too close for comfort. If you set it up half a mile away that can provide the distance that somehow enables both company spokespeople and journalists to develop a sense of proportion about what has happened.

CHECKLIST 8.2:
EQUIPMENT NEEDED IN A PRESS CENTRE

You should provide the following:

■ telephones (and extra lines, if necessary);

■ telex;

■ fax machine;

■ television;

■ video recorder (to record coverage of incident);

■ radio;

■ tape recorder (to tape radio coverage);

■ audio-visual aids (to explain background to incident);

■ typewriters;

■ stationery;

■ tea, coffee and soft drinks;

■ quiet room (for broadcast interviews).

You should remember that much of this equipment may need to be transported to site, so it needs to be readily accessible and transport must be instantly available.

3. Draft a briefing kit to use in the event of crisis

You won't have time to draft all the background documentation you will need if a crisis strikes, so you must arrange to have the task done in advance. The media will be hungry for information about your company, its products, its managers and any installations or other company activities that are directly involved in the crisis. The information you have already put into the Data Modules in this book could be particularly useful in this respect.

Normally it might seem like hard work trying to get journalists interested in your mission, business objectives, what you do and so on. But when a crisis strikes, it can seem as though every media newshound in the country and beyond is after the information.

Remember ... you need to be in a position to start providing information about your organization within minutes of a crisis occurring.

CHECKLIST 8.3:
WHAT TO INCLUDE IN A CRISIS BRIEFING KIT

You should include the following:

- details of the incident in bald, factual terms as far as is *definitely* known;

- background to the company;

- background to the installation involved in the crisis;

- what it does and the benefits it provides to the local community; and more broadly

- background to product(s) involved in the incident, who uses them and the benefits they provide; and

- details of senior managers involved in managing the company and the crisis incident.

You should also identify those media or special interest groups that are likely to display concern if a given crisis occurs. It is important to know who and how many journalists are likely to want information about the incident. And it is also important to know how to contact people such as political and community leaders, public officials and others who may want up-to-date information about the incident.

EIGHT WAYS TO GET FAIR-MINDED PEOPLE ON YOUR SIDE IN A CRISIS

It is when a corporate crisis strikes that your company is most likely to provoke critics – and when it most needs friends. It would be naïve to imagine that you can disarm all your critics in a crisis. People with an axe to grind will always find reason to carp. And a crisis tends to make your company a target for the release of pent-up feelings. But if you do the right things, you should win a hearing from fair-minded people.

Remember ... a crucial test of your success in crisis communications is whether you are winning or losing the support of fair-minded and unbiased people of goodwill.

Many of the points you have already picked up in this book apply as much in crisis communications as in other kinds of communications. But there are special features of crisis communications that you need to be aware of.

So, when a crisis strikes you need to be or do the following.

- **First with the news.** It's your crisis – and don't let anyone take it away from you! You must demonstrate that you are aware of what is happening. And if, in the early hours of the crisis, you are short of hard news, you should seek to fill the gap with relevant background material. By giving the press some facts, you may reduce their temptation to speculate.

- **The authoritative source of information.** When Perrier water was polluted with traces of benzene, the company didn't try to hide the facts. Instead, it announced itself what had gone wrong. By pinpointing the trouble as the use of sloppy bottling procedures by some workers, the company narrowed the scope of the problem and made the damage more containable. It also made itself the prime source of information about the incident – this stopped a great deal of uninformed and potentially damaging press speculation. The company announced without pressure that it was withdrawing its product. And when the problem was solved it was equally vigorous in saying so. You need to be the source from which the media gets the facts first. To do that, you need to demonstrate openness. You need to be truthful and accurate. Always tell the truth. As Oscar Wilde said: 'If you tell the truth sooner or later you'll be found out.' And you have to be prepared to release information as and when it becomes available. To do otherwise risks encouraging the media to seek other sources of information – sources that may be hostile to you. At the same time, while being helpful with information, you should rigorously avoid speculation about what *might* be happening. 'It's too early to say . . .' might be the true response and sounds reasonable and responsible.

- **Proactive in your response to the crisis.** That means not only being open and timely in releasing information about an incident, but also providing information as soon as possible about what you are going to do to rectify the situation. But don't hand hostages to fortune. Stick to the facts and what is actually about to be 'delivered'. In order to be first with the news, the authoritative source of information and proactive in its provision you should

- **Hold regular press conferences.** It helps to demonstrate you are willing to communicate. And it takes pressure off your spokespeople by stemming the flow of calls to the press centre from journalists. For every press conference prepare thoroughly. (It might be helpful to review Checklist 6.6 on press conferences again.) Set a reasonable time limit. Close the conference decisively when journalists have had a fair opportunity to ask their questions. Try to arrange for your spokespeople to leave by a separate exit from the journalists to avoid them being pursued by reporters, camera crews and photographers. But don't convey the impression that they're slinking away. At press conferences and in other meetings with the media and others involved with the crisis you should be

- **Concerned and compassionate.** You must demonstrate that you sympathize with people who have suffered as a result of the incident. Say so in any statement you make. Show real human warmth and understanding for their trouble. Don't appear like a cold, calculating, company hack. If you try 'smart' explanations to try and shift the blame you could alienate many people who recognize that accepting responsibility and showing sympathy is a more courageous and human response. When the Exxon Valdez ran aground in Prince William Sound, Alaska, spilling 11 million gallons of crude oil, its owners suffered massive damaging publicity. Exxon judged one of the most sensitive issues to be the damage to wildlife by the oil spill. The much-televised fate of sea otters was judged to be especially damaging. To counter this, the company spent $48m trying to save them. Fresh salmon was flown in from California to feed the besmirched animals. And 200 were saved at a cost of $40,000 each. Even so, the company will take years to recover from the incident – especially as it has given the language a new word. In the US, to 'Exxon' now means 'to make a mess of or behave clumsily'.

- **Able to refute false accusations about your company or the incident.** In a crisis, accusations can start to fly. They need to be put down as firmly as you know how (but whenever possible without rancour), as swiftly as possible. To leave accusations unanswered allows them to fester and become part of the mythology of an incident. The best way to put down accusations is with irrefutable facts. You need to make sure that any facts you need are going to be readily available. When Lever Brothers was accused of using an ingredient that aggravated skin diseases in one of its soap powders, the company defused the issue by arranging independent tests of its product by respected dermatologists.

- **Keep everyone affected by the incident informed.** That means keeping in direct contact with employees and families of employees. It also may mean keeping in direct contact with local councils, MPs and community leaders. You will be building goodwill after an incident by showing you are helpful and accessible to people who may have an interest or may take a view of the situation.

- **Match your emotions and message with the mood of the moment.** You need to demonstrate that you are aware of the feelings of people involved in the incident. You need to be more than a reciter of facts and figures about your company and the incident. You must demonstrate an appropriate emotional response in what you do and say. (But that doesn't mean you should indulge in insincere hand-wringing.) You need to be totally sincere and honest about your emotional response for it to ring true and be acceptable.

TO SUM UP

In this chapter you've:

- reviewed the four reasons why communicating in crisis is different from other forms of communication with the media;

- identified a list of questions to ask in order to identify the danger 'hot spots' in your company;

- reviewed how to set up a crisis command centre and a crisis press centre;

- identified the information that needs to be included in a crisis briefing kit;

- discovered eight things you need to do to get critics on your side in a crisis.

◀ 9 ▶

Learning From Experience

'Everything you read in the newspapers is absolutely true, except for the rare story of which you happen to have first-hand knowledge.'

Erwin Knoll, US newspaper editor

In 'Learning from Experience' you'll learn about:

- how to evaluate the results of your efforts as a spokesperson;
- how to measure the impact of your activities as a spokesperson;
- what to do when it all goes wrong.

HOW TO EVALUATE THE RESULTS OF YOUR EFFORTS AS A SPOKESPERSON

If you are to be effective as a company spokesperson, you will need to evaluate the impact of what you are doing. In performing this task you need to look at two issues:

- your personal performance as a spokesperson; and

- the impact of your efforts as a spokesperson upon your company's business objectives.

Let's now look at each of these issues in turn.

1. How effectively you perform as a spokesperson

You need to be as objective as possible about your own performance as a spokesperson. And, where possible, you should invite the constructive comments of helpful and trusted colleagues on your performance.

After every interview, try to answer these questions as honestly as possible. (If a colleague was present, you might ask his or her opinion on the same questions.)

- Did I manage to get across my main message during the interview?

- If not, why not:
    had I thought it through enough?
    did I explain it clearly enough?
    did I pitch it at the right level for the journalist?
    was my message backed with convincing facts?
    did I use enough illuminating examples?

- Did the interview serve either a specific business objective or the broader corporate objectives of the organization?

If you answer 'no' to any of these questions, you need to consider what you can do next time to improve that aspect of your performance. If you did louse up, these words might help: 'A man should never be ashamed to admit he has been in the wrong, which is but saying, in other words, that he is wiser today than he was yesterday', Alexander Pope.

2. Whether the results of the interview were helpful to your company's business objectives

In assessing whether you helped your company's business aims you need to be both objective and realistic. First, you need to appreciate that the media's primary purpose is not to help you achieve your business objectives. If necessary refer back to Chapter 1 to remind yourself about how the media approaches interviews and what drives journalists.

Secondly, most people do not read every article in every newspaper and magazine to which they subscribe with obsessive attention to detail. In general, they tend to leave an article with a 'general impression'. The same is true of most television and radio programmes. (If you asked someone to name three specific stories from yesterday's newspaper, they would probably be hard put to do it.) Today's newspaper is tomorrow's fish and chip wrapping.

So, in general, it is advisable to look at what has been written from the point of view of a mildly interested outsider. Would that outsider grasp the main thrust of your message? Would he generally think better of your company as a result of reading the article?

Don't be obsessed with minor errors of fact or subtle nuances of meaning which you think the writer has missed. The mildly interested reader is not going to be obsessed by them. Of one thing you can be certain: minor errors will occur frequently. In many cases, although regrettable, they don't make much difference to the overall main thrust of your message. So keep a sense of proportion about them. As Hollywood star Katharine Hepburn did. She said: 'I don't care what is written about me so long as it isn't true.'

Similarly, the interviewer may present your views in a slightly different way to that which you had hoped. Again, keep your feet on the ground. Be objective. Has the main point of your message really been missed? If not, you have probably achieved your main objective.

The exception to this reasonably relaxed approach to reviewing what is written about you is where you are hoping to direct very specific – and in some cases technical or semi-technical – messages to very specialist target audiences. In these cases, the detail of the presentation and the line taken can be more important.

> **Remember ...** if you become too obsessive about what is written about your company, you will fail to see the broader issues involved, you will rapidly become discouraged with your corporate communications and you will fail to achieve the many positive benefits that can flow from a constructive dialogue with the media.

In relating the results of media communications activity to business objectives, you need to develop relevant measures of success together with the machinery for monitoring those measures.

HOW TO MEASURE THE IMPACT OF YOUR ACTIVITIES AS A SPOKESPERSON

In measuring the results of your activities as a spokesperson, there are two main issues you need to address:

- how much media coverage you achieved – and whether it was helpful; and

- whether that coverage moved your company closer to achieving any of its business objectives.

The first is easier to measure than the second – but, with a certain amount of thought and ingenuity the second issue can also usefully be monitored.

Let's look at each in turn.

1. How much media coverage your activities have achieved

There are a number of approaches that you can adopt. They contain varying degrees of sophistication and may or may not be relevant depending on the precise circumstances of your campaign.

- **Column inches.** A crude measure, but one that can give you a warm feeling if there are plenty of cuttings. (For broadcast coverage, substitute minutes for inches.) The trouble is that not all coverage carries the same weight or is of equal value. And some of the coverage may not be positive. Some of it may not even be as a result of your activities. But don't write off column inches completely. They are proof that you have been doing something – and that it has had a result.

- **Weighted coverage.** This is one step – or, perhaps in some cases, two steps – up from counting the column inches. Instead you weight each cutting. You assign points for the type of journal (according to how precisely it reaches your target audiences) and how helpful the article is in putting across your message. You devise your own points scheme which reflects your own objectives and concerns. This helps to put some credible measure on the results of your activities. One computer services company that made extensive use of public relations valued the coverage it gained against the cost of buying the same advertising space in the publications concerned. Although that technique failed to take account of the fact that coverage was not always helpful, it showed that the money spent on PR was generally good value.

- **Audience-related coverage.** You measure the coverage you get against the likely proportion of your target audience reached by the media carrying the coverage. There is no precise scientific way of doing this. But by collating details of the circulation profiles of publications in which material on your company appears, and matching that against the total size of your audience, you can get a fair measure of whether or not you are hitting the right media.

2. Whether media coverage has helped to achieve business objectives

It is not easy to find a precise scientific way of measuring the contribution of a media communications campaign to specific business objectives. Clearly, the interplay of different forces affecting the achievement of any given objective could be so complex that it would be impossible to define precisely the influence of one from another.

But you can often get some measure of success. The starting point is to apply a methodology that is increasingly applied to the measurement of total business success – the use of *critical success factors* and *key performance indicators*.

The key to using this methodology successfully in measuring the impact of corporate communications is to choose relevant critical success factors for each business objective. Then you have to find a realistic key performance indicator or indicators for each critical success factor. And, finally, you need to devise machinery for relating the impact of your corporate communications campaign to the key performance indicator – the *measurement process*.

That can best be explained by the following two examples.

- **New product launch.** If you launch a new product in the capital goods market, a critical success factor might be how many you will sell in year one. A key performance indicator of whether you will achieve that is how many enquiries you receive about it from qualified prospective purchasers. It is possible to monitor the source of information – the measurement process – that generated those enquiries by telephone or questionnaire and determine how many came as a result of your media communications. For example, when it was set up, the Centre for the Study of the

Professions at Aston University, received more enquiries from press coverage than targeted mail shots. One Centre member commented: 'Bumf gets put in the in-tray for the odd spare moment. In the end, it gets binned. A news report makes something immediate. You feel compelled to respond in case the opportunity is a fleeting one and you miss the boat.'

- **Staff recruitment.** If your aim is to increase and improve the skill of your workforce, a critical success factor might be recruiting and retaining people with specific qualifications. In this case, a key performance indicator could be how many job applications you receive from qualified people in every quarter and how many existing qualified staff leave. If you are running a sustained corporate communications campaign aimed at potential and existing staff, the trend (the key performance indicator) revealed by new applicants and resignations (the measurement process) could be a reasonable guide to your success.

As you can see, each business objective will have its own critical success factor(s) which, in turn, require relevant key performance indicator(s).

Remember ... the true effectiveness of any media communications can only be judged by assessing its impact on those factors that will determine whether or not the objective is achieved.

You are now ready to try to define some measures for the impact your media communications campaign is having on your business objectives. You can use Data Module 20, on p 238, to do this.

In doing this for your company, you should refer back to Data Module 7 in Chapter 3, in which you listed your business objectives.

Now list those objectives again in Column 1 of Data Module 20.

In Column 2, list against each business objective the critical success factor(s) that will determine whether you achieve it or not. In Column 3, list any key performance indicator(s) that can help you measure whether you are achieving your critical success factor(s). And in Column 4, list the measurement process that will be used for each key performance indicator.

DATA MODULE 20: MEASURING THE IMPACT OF MEDIA
COMMUNICATIONS ON CORPORATE OBJECTIVES

Objective	Critical success factor	Key performance indicator	Measurement process
1.			
2.			
3.			
4.			
5.			
6.			
7.			

When you have completed Data Module 20, you will have mapped out:

- which business objectives are likely to be assisted by your media communications campaign;

- the ways in which you can measure that success.

When you have decided which key performance indicators you are going to measure, you will need to put in place the measurement process. There are a wide range of possible measurement processes. They include:

- market research studies;

- personal questioning;

- telephone surveys;

- postal surveys;

- desk research of existing performance data;

- discussion groups.

In measuring the impact of media communications, no method is perfect. But using any method concentrates the mind wonderfully on making sure that the activity serves defined objectives.

WHAT TO DO WHEN IT ALL GOES WRONG

One thing you can be sure of: mistakes will happen. What you need to do is to keep a sense of proportion about these mistakes. There are various courses of action open to you for correcting mistakes, but before you embark on any of them you should ask yourself whether any real harm has been done.

You may well find yourself dealing with journalists from certain publications that regularly cover your industry area. It doesn't help long-term relations to be carping continually about minor errors. Indeed, when something *does* go wrong, you should always start by asking whether it was possibly your fault. Did you explain it clearly enough? Did you provide the right information? A surprising number of 'mistakes' in newspapers and magazines occur because journalists were given the 'wrong' information. However, as American presidential candidate, Senator Adlai Stevenson said: 'Accuracy to a newspaper is what virtue is to a lady, but a newspaper can always print a retraction.'

If something has gone wrong, there are a number of possible ways to put it right, as follows.

A 'quiet word'

Start by approaching the journalist who has made the mistake. The mistake may – indeed often will – be completely innocent and he or she will be anxious to put it right. Your approach should be friendly rather than censorious. In some cases, you will find the journalist is pleased that you have approached him or her first rather than going direct to the editor. You may find the journalist willing to write a 'follow-on' story (see below), in which the original error can be corrected as well as new information given. Clearly, if the journalist is unhelpful, and you feel the matter is sufficiently important, you must approach the editor for a correction.

A correction

You should ask for a correction where there has been a significant error of fact. When doing so, ask for the correction as soon as possible. Give the editor as much time as you can to get it into the next issue of the paper. And make sure your facts are absolutely correct when asking for the correction. But be certain the correction will not do more harm than good, as this correction from the Scottish newspaper, the *Dunoon Observer*, possibly did: 'The old pouffe which started the fire at number seven, Douglas Cottages, as reported last week, referred to an item of furniture and not the owner, Mr Donnie McArthur.'

The editor may publish the correction in one of two ways.

- As a formal correction, normally an item on the same or a page near to where the original article appeared. And the correction may or may not offer an apology according to whether or not any serious inconvenience or hurt was caused. For example, *The Independent* published the following formal correction on 3 July 1989: 'Due to a transcription error, an article in Saturday's *Independent* on page 2 on Irish premier Charles Haughey mistakenly read "a man of immense rudeness". This was intended to read "a man of great shrewdness".' In the best traditions, the correction was also published on page 2.

● As a follow-on story. What journalists call correcting the error 'in passing'. The journalist will mention the error in his new story and give the true facts. It will generally be done in a downbeat way.

Letter to the editor

You should use a letter to the editor where you feel that the publication has seriously misrepresented your point of view. When the *Financial Times* attacked the present system for fixing the charges of international telephone calls, British Telecom chairman, Iain Vallance, moved fast to put his point of view. He wrote a letter to the editor which appeared the next day. Three lessons can be learned from the Vallance letter: 1. the faster you reply, the more likely your letter will be published; 2. the more senior the writer, the more likely it will be used; 3. a reasoned reply is worth the column inches it occupies. (The letter to the editor can be used for serious errors of fact, but these are best dealt with by the method described above.) When correcting what the writer has originally written, do so in a constructive way. And try to write without rancour or name-calling which does not normally enhance your case. Stick to the central issues where you feel misrepresented, and make sure your letter is crystal clear. Don't make it sound like a letter from a solicitor. Keep the tone polite and businesslike.

Appeal to a newspaper ombudsman

In response to mounting criticism about sensationalism and invasion of privacy, most of the national press adopted a five-point code of conduct in December 1989. To support the implementation of that code, and to provide more effective machinery for dealing with reader's complaints, most national newspapers have now appointed ombudsmen. At the time of going to press, newspaper ombudsmen, or 'readers' representatives' as some are called, were: *Sun* – Ken Donlan; *Star* – Maurice Richards; *Daily Express* – Tony Fowler; *Daily Mail/Mail on Sunday* – Chris Rees; *Today* – Robert Edwards; *Daily Mirror/Sunday Mirror/People* – Peter Archer MP; *The Times* – John Grant; *Daily Telegraph/Sunday Telegraph* – Ricky Marsh; *Guardian* – Hugh Stephenson; *The Independent* – Sir Gordon Downey; *Observer* – Adam Raphael; *Sunday Express* – Max Davidson; *News of the World* – Phil Wrack; *Independent on Sunday* – Owen Hickey; *Evening Standard* – Vyvyan Harmsworth; *Daily Record (Glasgow)* – Tom Carbery; *Sunday Times* – Charles Wintour. In some cases, these are journalists on the paper, in others figures from outside the newspaper industry.

In most cases, you will get best results if you seek any correction from the editor first. But where this is not forthcoming, an appeal to the newspaper ombudsman could be worthwhile. Placing your case before a newspaper ombudsman does not preclude you from also complaining to the Press Complaints Commission or taking any other course of action.

Complaint to the Press Complaints Commission

At the beginning of 1991, the Press Council was abolished and replaced with a new body, the Press Complaints Commission (PCC). The PCC operates from the same offices as the old Press Council and has the same director – Kenneth Morgan. The Commission has 15 members – seven editors, two former editors, and six others – plus its chairman.

The old Press Council had been called 'toothless'. In recent years, there has been growing concern about press 'misbehaviour', invasion of privacy and unwarranted sensationalism. These and other charges were investigated in 1989–90 by the Calcutt Committee which recommended setting up the new body.

The hope is that the PCC will encourage the observance of more responsible newspaper conduct. Only time will tell, and at the time of writing, the PCC was still establishing its complaints procedures.

In outline, if you wish to make a complaint to the PCC, the procedure is as follows.

- First, try to get the matter corrected by the offending publication – it's the quickest and easiest way.

- If that doesn't succeed, send details of your complaint, together with a copy of the offending article, to the director of the PCC. You can only complain if you have been directly affected by the article concerned. In other words, you cannot complain on behalf of a third party.

- The director will send your complaint to the editor of the publication. The editor may respond to you directly and may print a correction or retraction.

- But if the editor's response does not satisfy you, the PCC may consider the complaint further. In this case, the director will draft an adjudication and send it to the members of the commission. Only if they disagree with it, will the complaint be debated at the PCC's monthly meeting, after which a final adjudication will be made.

- The editor of the offending publication may publish the adjudication or a summary of it. But this is not mandatory. Lord McGregor, current chairman of the PCC, has said: 'I'm not particularly interested in censure or how it's published. I'm interested in getting the [PCC] Code observed and trying to develop a confidence between the Press and the people.'

The Press Complaints Commission has adopted a new Code of Conduct, designed to provide guidelines to the Press. (Copies are available from the PCC.) The code has no force in law, but is taken into consideration when complaints are considered. So, in making a complaint, it could be useful to refer to those sections of the code you believe have been breached. A significant feature of the code is that it should be observed 'in the spirit as well as the letter'. Those points from the code which could be relevant to executives and companies include the following.

- **Accuracy.** Publications must take care to be accurate. When they have made a mistake or published distorted or misleading material, they should correct it promptly and with 'due prominence'. They should add an apology 'whenever appropriate'.

- **Right of reply.** There should be a fair opportunity for individuals and organizations.

- **Subterfuge.** Journalists should not obtain information through misrepresentation. They should not take documents or photographs without the owner's consent. But they may breach these requirements when it is in the 'public interest' to do so. That includes:
    detecting or exposing crime or serious misdemeanour;
    detecting or exposing anti-social conduct;
    protecting public health or safety;
    preventing the public being misled by some statement or action of an individual or organization.

- **Harassment.** Journalists shouldn't harass. With the exception of the public interest let-out, they shouldn't photograph you on private property without your permission; they should leave the property when asked and should not continue to telephone when asked to stop.

- **Financial journalism.** Journalists should not make a profit out of information they receive in advance of publication, even when the law does not prohibit it. They shouldn't pass information on to others either. They shouldn't write about stocks and shares in which they or their close family members have an interest, nor trade in shares they have recently tipped or plan to tip.

- **Confidentiality.** Journalists have a 'moral obligation' to protect sources.

The address of the Press Complaints Commission is No 1, Salisbury Court, London EC4Y 8AE.

Complaint about a television or radio programme

If you want to complain about a television or radio programme, you should first send your complaint to the person responsible for the programme concerned. In the case of news broadcasts, this will be the editor. In the case of documentaries or 'magazine'-type programmes, it will be the producer. If you are not satisfied with their response you can complain to the managing director of BBC Television or BBC Radio, the Independent Broadcasting Authority or the Cable Authority, as relevant. In cases of clear, demonstrable and major error, the broadcasting companies are normally prepared to broadcast a correction. But they are frequently unwilling to broadcast corrections for small but possibly significant errors.

Complaint to the Broadcasting Complaints Commission

If you are not satisfied with the response of the BBC, the Independent Broadcasting Authority or the Cable Authority, you can make a complaint to the Broadcasting Complaints Commission. The commission considers complaints of unjust or unfair treatment in radio, television or cable programmes. It also considers complaints of unwarranted infringement of privacy in or in connection with such programmes. Complaints include advertisements, teletext services and the broadcasts of the BBC World Service.

If you wish to make a complaint the procedure is as follows.

- First, you can only make a complaint if you were actually a participant in the programme or were directly affected by it. Companies can make complaints. An example is when BBC Television's *Watchdog* programme criticized (in 1990) major oil companies for making excessive profits, Shell UK sought a correction from the BBC. The BBC refused so Shell went to the Broadcasting Complaints Commission. The *Watchdog* programme had said that the petrol industry was not competitive, that major oil producers had increased their number of outlets in recent years, and that petrol prices went up quickly when oil costs rose, but fell slowly when oil costs declined. Shell UK cited a report from the Monopolies and Mergers Commission to show those claims were false. The Broadcasting Complaints Commission found for Shell and the BBC broadcast a 480-word correction on BBC1 and BBC2 and published it in the *Radio Times*. Afterwards, the BBC said: 'It is an honourable apology. We realized we got it wrong and said so.'

- You can only make a complaint after approaching the BBC, Independent Broadcasting Authority or Cable Authority direct. You should make your complaint in writing and include the title of the relevant programme, the date and channel on which it was broadcast and the precise nature of your complaint.

- The commission will only consider your complaint if:

    the unjust or unfair treatment or infringement of privacy you're complaining about is not the subject of legal proceedings in the UK;
    you do not have a remedy by way of legal proceedings;
    it is not frivolous;
    you have made the complaint within a reasonable time of the broadcast.

- If the commission decides to consider your complaint, it sends a copy to the relevant broadcasting authority and also seeks a copy of the transcript and a written response to your complaint. If an independent programme maker is concerned, it is sent a copy of your complaint via either the Independent Broadcasting Authority or the Cable Authority.

- When the commission receives the broadcaster's comments,

it may give you the chance to comment on them. Then the broadcaster gets the chance to comment on your comments.

- It is also possible that you could be invited to a private hearing at which the broadcasters will also be present. The main purpose of the hearing is to get additional information about your complaint and the broadcaster's response. In some cases, the commission will see each side separately.

- Following that process, which can take several weeks, the commission reaches its findings. It normally instructs the broadcasting body to broadcast its findings and to publish them in either the *Radio Times* or *TV Times*. It does this whether or not the complaint has been upheld. But the commission cannot force the broadcasters to apologize, broadcast a correction or compensate for loss.

- The Broadcasting Complaints Commission publishes a full set of guidance notes on making a complaint, and also an annual report detailing complaints that it has dealt with during the past year. It is available from the Broadcasting Complaints Commission, Grosvenor Gardens House, 35–37 Grosvenor Gardens, London SW1W 0BS.

Complaint to the Broadcasting Standards Authority

This body handles complaints about the screen portrayal of violence, sex and standards of taste and decency. Its remit covers TV advertising, radio and videos. If it considers a serious issue is at stake, it will hold a hearing and arrange for its findings to be publicized. The address of the Broadcasting Standards Authority is 5–8 The Sanctuary, London SW1P 3JS.

Issue a writ for libel

This is definitely a last resort. And you should not take action at all unless you consult a lawyer. Incidentally, when it comes to libel, it does no harm to consult one of the firms of specialist libel lawyers who still cluster around Fleet Street even though the newspapers have left – the publication you are suing will probably be doing the same. You certainly don't want to be outgunned on the legal front.

In order to prove libel, you have to establish the following.

- That what you're complaining about was actually published. In this context, published means also broadcast on radio, television or teletext. It is also worth noting that you can be libelled in a picture as well as words. When a magazine published an article about Christmas thieving at Smithfield market, it illustrated the piece with a picture of a market porter taking part in the annual meat-carrying race. He collected £1,500 in damages.

- That it refers to you or your company. It doesn't necessarily have to refer to you by name, but you or your company must be recognizable from what is written. For example, in 1984, the *Daily Telegraph* published an article saying that the affairs of a Lloyd's insurance syndicate were under investigation following heavy losses. The article suggested that three underwriters were facing 'criminal proceedings'. Although the underwriters were not named, they were clearly identifiable by anyone in the know. Two of them collected damages of £37,500 and £32,500, respectively.

- That what is written about you or your company is defamatory. There are three tests as to whether something might be defamatory. They are:
  - whether what you complain of tends to lower you in the estimation of right-thinking members of society;*
  - whether it tends to bring you into hatred, ridicule,

---

* As, for example, Lord Weinstock, managing director of GEC was, when the *New Scientist* accused him wrongfully of trying to influence the government against improving the status of engineers. Damages: £40,000.

contempt, dislike or disesteem with those right thinkers;**

- whether it tends to make you shunned or avoided or cut off from the said right thinkers.

You could find that the people you are suing for libel will try one of five defences.

- **Justification.** If what was written was true they have a complete answer to your charge of defamation.

- **Fair comment.** If the writer of the offending article can show that what was said was his or her honest opinion, made without malice, then you may lose your case.

- **Privilege.** Some things can be published and receive complete protection from suits for libel. They include reports of judicial proceedings and parliamentary papers. Fair and accurate reports of them in publications also attract privilege. So, in some cases, do fair and accurate reports of public meetings.

- **Section 4 of the Defamation Act 1952.** The publisher of the libel can claim that it was 'innocent' – the publisher did not mean to publish the libel about you and did not know of the circumstances in which what was written referred to you. But the publisher must have taken 'reasonable care' and he must make a prompt offer of 'amends' after his unwitting libel.

- **Apology under the Libel Acts 1843 and 1845.** Very rare. Only applies to newspapers and periodicals. The publisher must show that the libel got into the paper without malice or negligence and that he or she apologized or offered to apologize as soon as the mistake was realized.

But always remember that libel is certainly a last resort. A case can

** As Ingham Engineering, a Renault car specialist, was when wrongfully accused in a car magazine of being 'a fairly unspeakable bunch of grease monkeys'. Damages: £5,000.

last for days, if not weeks, with vast costs. When a Harley Street doctor who specializes in slimming treatments was wrongfully accused on the BBC's *That's Life* programme of being a 'profiteering unscrupulous quack', he sued the BBC. The trial lasted for 87 days, after which the BBC paid agreed damages of £75,000. Costs – also paid by the BBC – were estimated at £1m.

And even if you win, you may only score a pyrrhic victory. As did the unhappy legal executive who sued the *Sunday Express*. He had tried to avoid parking tickets by registering his car in his small son's name. The *Sunday Express* described him as 'a slippery unscrupulous spiv'. At the first trial he won £12,000 damages. But that was set aside by the Court of Appeal. At the second trial, his damages were set at just ½p – the smallest coin of the realm. And he had to pay all the first trial costs, the appeal costs and most of the second trial costs.

THE NEXT STEPS

Well, that's it. You have finally come to the end of *The Complete Spokesperson*. If you have been through every page and completed every data module, you must be congratulated for your thoroughness – not to mention your feat of endurance! But, where do you go from here?

1. You cannot expect to absorb every fact and piece of advice in *The Complete Spokesperson* at once. From time to time, return to those chapters of the book you feel are relevant to whatever work you have in hand.

2. Don't just put your copy of *The Complete Spokesperson* up on a shelf to gather dust. It is intended as more than a once-only source of instruction. It should be a useful source of reference. You can use the checklists as ideal quick reminders before undertaking a particular media assignment. And the completed Data Modules should be a ready source of information about your own company's media policy.

3. Put the lessons you have learned into effect. It is not a detailed

knowledge of theory, but practical experience that is going to make you a valuable spokesperson for your organization.

4. Don't expect to achieve miracles overnight. Building a corporate personality and getting across key company messages takes time. And it requires persistence. So does building useful and productive media contacts. Don't be put off by the occasional rebuff.

5. Whatever your specialist management discipline – and it might, of course, be communications or public relations – you could find that the ability to communicate well-conceived and expressed messages will give a valuable boost to your career prospects.

If you have found *The Complete Spokesperson* useful, you might want to practise what you have learned. Policy Consultants, run by the authors of the book, run a flexible range of training workshops that enable managers to develop media communication planning and media presentation skills further. Details are available from Policy Consultants, 29 Tivoli Road, Brighton, East Sussex BN1 5BG. Tel: 0273 565505.

Remember, we are entering the Age of the Communicator. Good luck!

THE COMPLETE SPOKESPERSON

In this chapter you've:

- found out the questions to ask to evaluate your success as a company spokesperson;

- discovered three different ways to measure the amount of media coverage generated by your efforts;

- reviewed a methodology for measuring the effectiveness of your media communications in achieving defined business objectives;

- applied that methodology to your own circumstances;

- reviewed the different actions you can take when the media gets your message wrong.

Index